Systems Thinking
and
The Logic of Tao Philosophy

Systems Thinking
and
The Logic of Tao philosophy

November 23, 2021

By

Wayne L. Wang PH.D.

Helena Island Publisher

2021

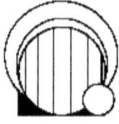

Published by

Helena Island Publisher
Darien, Illinois, USA 60561

Copyright ©2016 by Wayne L. Wang

This book is printed by Print-on-Demand technology
So its contents are updated regularly.

Printed in the United States of America
November 23, 2021

Wang, Wayne L., 1944 -
Systems Thinking and The Logic of Tao Philosophy
/by Wayne L. Wang
(A Searching for Tao Series Volume 7)
Includes bibliographical references

Systems Thinking
Tao Philosophy

Cover Graphic: *Tao: 1-2-3* by Wayne L. Wang

This book serves as a complement to the *Logic of Tao Philosophy*, which has been under development for over a decade by the author. I have relaced the *Searching for Tao Series* with the *Nature Independence Thinking Series* because the latter has been developed with a coherent series. The *Series* has been in the form of self-publishing so they are updated regularly relying on the comments and online communications for improvement.

The author will continue to improve the quality of the presentation, so the books are update-to-date. The Series now covers a sufficient spectrum of the issues related to the logic of Tao philosophy, including its relations to other ancient philosophies, religion, psychotherapy, and systems thinking. The books in this *Series* will continue to develop with feedback from the audience.

DEDICATION

To the memory of

My Parents
Wang Tien-hai and Yu Ah-lung
王天海　王游阿弄

And

My Brother
Shi-yuen Wang
王西源

NATURE INDEPENDENCE SERIES

Nature Independence Series is to provide the theoretical basis and ability to establish new Laozi philosophy. All editions are bilingual, a few with English-only versions.

The reference and this book are available at www.amazon.com as eBook, paperback, and hardcover. The book abstracts are in https://dynamictaos.com.

CONTENTS

Table of Equations

TABLE OF FIGURES

PREFACE

The purpose of this work is to discuss the relationship between systems thinking and the logic of Tao philosophy. We show that Tao philosophy, along with many other ancient philosophies, may be understood in terms of systems. Systems view is another good way to understand the logic of Tao philosophy.

Systems thinking has become a platform to discuss science, living organisms, sociology, and psychology, and philosophy. Reality may be considered as a complex system of various concepts. Both systems and reality are based on the concept of wholeness. A reality is self-making and self-preserving like a living system.

Systems thinking is a complex issue and has been recently reviewed in great detail by Capra and Luisi. The theme was first introduced by Bertalanffy and Bogdanov in the 1920s. Readers may refer to Capra and Luisi for the complexity of systems thinking. We shall only be interested in the very basic characteristics of systems thinking. We are concerned only with the logic in the way we think of nature and the systems.

A systems theory starts with the function of a system and then identifies the network of the subsystems to support the function. This is rather similar to the philosophical inquiry about reality, where we think of reality and identify the propositions that can support reality.

In philosophy, the study of reality is called *ontology*. Reality has the goal to sustain as a living system. Both reality and living systems have a common goal of survival and rely on the networked subsystems to support this goal. Both have to support the wholeness of the system.

Philosophical subsystems are the underlying propositions that can be used to support the argument for a reality. Therefore, the reality is also a complex of networks of subsystems of many levels. The bottom level is the abstracted *objects of knowledge* (i.e. words) used to express the ideas used in our communications. These words form ideas and these ideas are networked together to describe reality. These objects are parts and the reality is the whole, so the philosophical system is a logical network of objects that support the reality.

Therefore, reality and systems have a common feature: both strive for "eternal" and independent existence. The existence of an entity means it has wholeness or Oneness – i.e., it is independent and free of external interactions. These entities are like living organisms. We shall discuss their common logic structure.

Scientific thinking on the surface may look different. It tries to validate the existence of the objects and then show the properties of the system in terms of the properties of the objects and their relations (interactions). Scientific theory plays an important role to integrate these objects. We shall show how the core concepts of systems and scientific thinking are interrelated.

Reality must be whole. The wholeness view is based on the Oneness of the system, which is a coherent complex of highly interconnected phenomena. The fundamental principle for both systems and scientific thinking is the *Principle of Oneness.* This principle ensures that our thinking is kept within the scope of reality.

In systems thinking, reality is a complex system that has a set of objects which together form the patterns of organization. Each reality is represented as an organic form or pattern consisting of objects. The patterns can represent the system. We were driven in this direction by the paradoxical words of Laozi.

We first encounter the principle of Oneness in the logical structure in Tao philosophy as a way to overcome the traditional dualistic interpretation of the *Tao Te Ching.* Tao philosophy may be considered as an ancient version of systems thinking. We may also find similar thinking in the Pre-Socratic and Indian philosophies. Systems thinking is an alternative way of looking at the Oneness of nature.

The logical structure of Tao philosophy is not new. It may be shown as the structure of the Square of Opposition that was discussed by Aristotle.

We often say that systems thinking in sciences started when we realize that the subatomic particles may have no meaning as isolated objects. The reality in the quantum world can be understood only as interconnections, or correlations, among various processes of observation and measurement.

Science has been quite successful in constructing from objects which may not have reality by themselves. Systems thinking also has been very successful in constructing reality from patterns of objects without relying on the properties of the objects. Philosophy also covers both realms; we have familiar realism and idealism. The approach of realism is similar to scientific thinking and idealism to systems thinking. However, behind all these obvious differences there is a common principle.

Chapter 1 Introduction

We make up our minds to name two modes of manifestation for a reality ... We must not treat the two modes as two separate and independent realities; otherwise, we will go astray.

Parmenides

General systems theory is the scientific exploration of the structure and wholeness of the systems. All systems form because of interactions between the parts; however, we cannot decompose the system into independently existing parts. A system is always a complex of many interacting subsystems. Systems theory tries to deal with these highly complex systems.

A very comprehensive review of the history and topic in the systems view of life is given in a new book by Professor Fritjof Capra and Pier Luigi Luisi.

The Logic of Tao Philosophy

It is easier for our discussion of systems theory first to define the logic of Tao philosophy. It is completely in the logical structure of the first chapter of the Tao Te Ching. I use the following paragraph structure:

1 Tao may be spoken of, but it is not the Heng Tao.
  Names may be named, but they are not Heng Names.
2 In the beginning, the myriad things are Wu the same;
  After being born, the myriad things are Yu different.
3 However,
  In Heng Wu, we, however, observe a subtle difference;
  In Heng Yu, we however observe fading boundaries.
4 Both states appear simultaneously, as
  Different manifestations of the same (Tao)
5 Profound upon profound,
  They are the gateways to all mysteries.

Systems Thinking

Each system has three things: (1) the purpose or function; (2) the elements; and (3) the interconnections.

The purpose is Heng Tao, the proper order of nature for the myriad things. The elements are the two opposites, Wu and Yu. The interconnection is not explicitly shown, but the effects of the interconnections result in Heng Wu and Heng Yu. The two opposites constitute the whole system. Wu and Yu are mixed due to interconnections in Heng Wu and Heng Yu.

We shall call the elements as *objects* in the model, the final results of interconnections, Heng Wu and Heng Yu, as the *actualities*.

When the final actualities are reached, there are no interactions between the actualities. These final actualities represent the final purpose. Systems theory refers to a system interacting with other systems which are before the final system is reached.

In the *Tao Te Ching*, the interconnection between the objects is represented as Chi 氣 which is invisible. The only purpose of this interaction is to preserve the principle of Tao in forming the actuality so that each actuality can represent the principle of Tao. In Tao philosophy, we also identify the principle of interaction as *Te* 德 which is obeyed by the interactions according to the principle of Tao.

The wholeness concept is represented by Heng 恆. The purpose is to achieve Heng or wholeness or a system view. In Tao, the myriad things should obey the unity of nature, which is called Tao.

The Logical Structure of Laozi

We may describe the wholeness of the myriad things by (1) two interconnected opposite objects Wu and Yu or by (2) the whole actualities. Both systems comprise the whole domain of Heng Tao.

We may the structure of From Chapter 1 as follows:

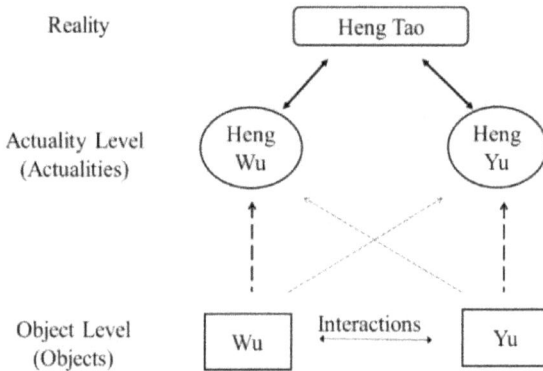

Figure 1 Basic Logical Structure of Laozi

This is a general description of "unity of opposition". The opposites are the objects and the principle of unity is Heng Tao. In the model, the harmonizing relationship between two objects is represented by an interaction.

We discuss reality at three levels. The absolute reality is the Tao itself or the function of the system. This function may be described at two levels. Sometimes, the object level is called the "hard" system and the actuality level is the "soft" system. In a hard system, we view the world as a cluster of interdependent systems; in a soft system, the characteristic of actuality is determined by the interconnected structure of objects. This is an important concept.

Definition of Systems

The main characteristics of systemic thinking emerged in Europe by biologists. Bogdanov and Bertalanffy independently formulated a comprehensive theoretical framework describing the principles of organization of living systems. The concept was further enriched in psychology, sociology, ecology, and physics, etc. Systems thinking has become very general.

We may try to treat any sustaining system as a living system. This is a common background thought in systems thinking, philosophy, and religions. The living systems and philosophical thinking of reality share the same characteristics of self-making and self-sustaining.

A system is a set of objects that are interconnected to produce patterns of behavior. These patterns serve to support the functions of the system. In philosophy, the reality is a set of thoughts that are linked to producing representations of reality. A general system can be a culture, a society, a religion, or any organization. The world is a living system.

Here we want to show that the systems thinking may be based on the principle of Oneness. In dualism, we describe a system with two opposite parts that cover the whole domain. These parts interact coherently to form patterns that can represent the characteristics of that system.

In our model, the system may be represented by two patterns. The two patterns have different characteristics and will appear at the same time and are two equivalent ways of representing the system. Thus, the system manifests in multiple ways but remains as indivisible.

We have to define a few terms so our discussion can be understood with consistency. For example, we need to define our concepts of "one and many" related to reality. A system is a coherent whole that has parts, but the system is constraint overall by the property of Oneness. We first adopt the following definitions:

- The Parts and the Incoherent Whole - A system has a whole domain subdivided into parts. Each part covers a non-overlapping subdomain. In terms of domains, the sum of the parts is the whole, but this whole is an uncorrelated whole where there is no correlation between the parts.

- Wholeness and Oneness - When all parts are fully interconnected, we say that the system has wholeness. The difference between wholeness and Oneness is that wholeness may have parts and Oneness is without any part. Therefore, we may have many subsystems with different structures of parts that constitute the same wholeness.
- In general, there are many patterns of objects that can form a coherent whole. These patterns may have different objects or different structures of objects, but they all form the same coherent whole.

In our discussions, each element is an object. The whole is the representation of Oneness in the phenomenal world. Oneness, commonly labeled as One by Plato or Parmenides, is infinite or indefinite. As described by Parmenides: "One then is neither at rest nor in motion." Oneness is beyond any multiplicity. One is not many, and therefore has no parts, and therefore, is not a whole, which is a sum of parts and therefore has neither beginning, middle, nor end, and is therefore unlimited, and therefore formless…"

Oneness is the transcendental characteristic of all systems in the phenomenal world.[1] A system must consist of three kinds of things: objects, interconnections, and the function or purpose of the system. The common purpose is to survive or to last like a living organism. For this purpose, the function is to maintain the wholeness where all parts are properly networked as in the system.

Two Equivalent Views on Systems

There are two ways to look at the systems: The objects view and the wholeness systems view. These two are often taken to be opposite views. But they are actually equivalent.

Science believes that, in any complex system, the behaviors of the whole could be analyzed in terms of the properties of its parts. In this mechanistic view, the world is a collection of interconnected objects. These objects interact with one another to support the function. In such science, the objects are of primary interest and the interconnections are secondary to show the properties of the system. Sometimes, this is called the Hard Systems view.

---

[1] Therefore, there is no Oneness in the phemomenal world. What can be described is wholeness, which cannot be Oneness. Laozi says, "Tao may be spoken of, but it is not the Heng Tao. 道可道，非恆道。"

For systems thinkers, the properties of the systems are the relations or the patterns of interconnected objects. Systems science shows that living systems cannot be understood by the analysis of the properties of objects. The properties of the parts inside the system are not intrinsic properties of the system. A part is merely used to build a pattern to support the properties of the system. The relationships of the objects are primary. These parts are not real. This is called the Soft Systems view.

A philosophical reality is also a network of relationships. Our descriptions of reality may be based on objects (words as names), but these objects are used only to form an interconnected network of concepts. The objects cannot represent reality.[1] In systems thinking, there is no definite building block of objects as long as the objects can form the patterns.

The two views have been successful approaches to understanding a system.

The Elements are Complementary

In our logic model, there is no real conflict between these two views. This is supported by Buddhism and Western philosophy (See References).

---

[1] As Laozi says, "Names may be named, but they are not Heng Names. 名可名，非恆名。"

They are complementary with the same principle. The logic relies on the interactions between the objects to build the patterns and the interactions between the patterns, while the logic of the system relies directly on the feedback interactions between the patterns. The interactions between the objects are responsible for creating the patterns and the feedbacks. We may show these two views in Figure 1:

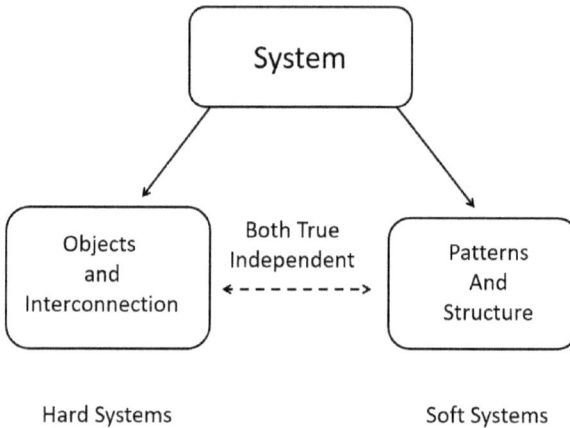

Figure 2 Two Systems Views

The hard systems view has dominated all our thinking for several hundred years, it is well-ingrained into our language and our description of reality is always language-dependent. It is still the only way we can describe nature.

Systems thinking try to free us from such thinking by pointing out that the elements are not real and we should maintain the wholeness preserved in the patterns. Systems thinking is a proper way to restore holistic thinking in many disciplines.

We shall concentrate on the common features in these two approaches. These two views are different representations of the same system. Both views should obey the same principle of wholeness or the principle of Oneness. Both views are equivalent.

In the following, we shall discuss the introductory background for our formal logic model, which is discussed in Chapter 3.

The Logical Structure of Systems

We shall define the structure of our logic model and the terminology to be used in our discussions. The basic structure is in Figure 1. For general systems discussions, we may extend it in Figure 3. The results of this simple model can shed important light on our discussions extrapolated to a general system.

We shall show the logic structure of the systems in terms of *objects*, *subsystems*, and the *final subsystems*. Therefore, they are the three levels in our model, as shown in Figure 3:

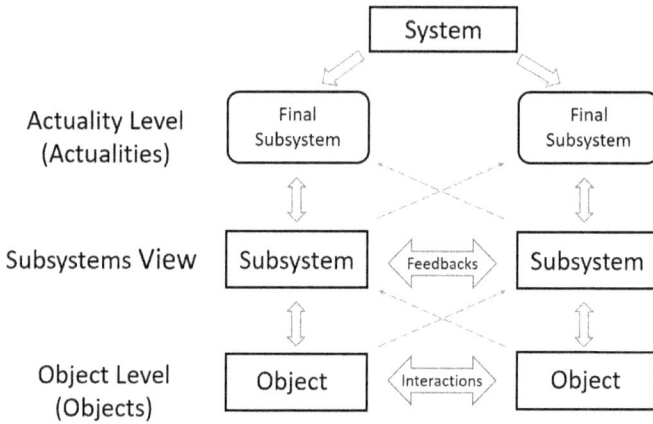

Figure 3 Three-Level Systems Thinking

At the object level, the system is represented by the objects and their interactions. Systems thinking is often at the subsystems level, where the subsystems support the function of the system with the mutual feedback interactions between the subsystems.

In a philosophical investigation of reality, the crucial question is: What is the reality? Whatever has interactions with its environment is not independent and therefore is not the ultimate reality. The reality is represented only at the actuality level, where the subsystems are fully integrated and become independent from each other. We shall call these final subsystems the *actualities* in our model. They are the true manifestations of the system.[1]

Therefore, the three levels in our model correspond to the hard and soft systems view and the philosophical view on reality. The final subsystems can represent reality in terms of the patterns of the subsystems or the objects. The actualities are the representations of reality in the phenomenal world.

Systems Thinking

Our systems thinking includes all levels shown in Figure 2. Traditional systems thinking is mainly concerned with the subsystems level with subsystems in their environments.[2] Each subsystem consists of a *subset* of the objects in the system, but the final subsystems contain all objects in the system.

---

[1]   It is like the monads of Leibniz.

[2]   Chinese holistic medicine may be an exception since all organs are interconnected. Each organ can represent the whole body. In our terminology, each organ is a fully integrated subsystem, i.e., an actuality.

As in metaphysics of reality, the final subsystems may be treated as manifestations or revelations of reality. As shown in Figure 2, when all objects are integrated to form the final representations of reality, we will have two, not one, final subsystems and each final subsystem is a holistic (and thus realistic) manifestation of the reality.

Objects and Language

Our description of the subsystems and the actualities are based on the objects. The objects are coded in our language. Our descriptions are language-dependent, but they will describe the same reality in different patterns of languages or different languages. The ultimate descriptions of the actualities are patterns of objects.

The patterns reflect the logical structure of the objects. Therefore, the logic of the system is the way we can use the objects to describe the actualities. If we understand the logic, then we may be able to construct the proper patterns of the language that can represent reality.

Three Levels are Equivalent

We should note that the three levels in Figure 2 are not three different levels of reality. At the actuality level, we describe the system in terms of actualities. At the subsystem level, we describe the system in terms of subsystems and their feedback interactions. At the object levels, we describe the system in terms of objects and their interactions.

The system is fully, completely, and equivalently represented at each level. In other words, each level should equally preserve the wholeness of the system. This is required by the principle of Oneness.

Since our tool for description is our objects of knowledge (language), the descriptions at all levels are eventually based on patterns of objects. The patterns are only implicit at the object level as the interconnectedness of the objects is governed by the laws of interactions.

Objects, Subsystems, and Actualities

To make our model clear, we shall further describe the *objects*, *subsystems*, and *actualities* used in our model. Ultimately, our inquires of the systems concern the relationship between the parts and the whole. This system is One; the realistic descriptions of the system must be whole. This has been the basic philosophical issue since Aristotle labeled it as the problem of "the one and the many."

Parts may be Objects or Subsystems

In our model, we define the "parts" as the *isolated* objects at the object level or the isolated subsystems at the subsystems level. Such isolations exclude the interactions between the objects or the feedback interactions between the subsystems. In terms of domain, the whole refers to the whole domain and each part belongs to a subdomain.

These isolated parts are interconnected via interactions. The interactions are external to the parts. Each part adapts to its environment and behaves as an autonomy by interacting with all other parts.

Internal and External Interactions

A subsystem is formed by a sub-group of objects in the system. The sub-groups may overlap. That is, an object may repeat in multiple subsystems as a member of different patterns. The objects in a subsystem interact with the objects in other subsystems. Here we categorize the interactions of the objects as *internal* and *external* interactions. The *internal interactions* are interactions between the objects inside the subsystem. Such internal interactions form the patterns of the subsystems. All interactions with the objects outside the subsystem are *external interactions.* The external interactions are reflected in the environment of the subsystem and constitute the feedback interactions.

Actualities

As more and more external interactions are internalized, the subsystems will involve more and more objects. Eventually, each final subsystem will contain all the objects in the system. Therefore, each final subsystem is a particular pattern of all objects in the system.

The final subsystem contains all interactions of all objects and there is no external interaction between the final subsystems. The final subsystem is the actualities in our model discussions.

Each actuality contains all objects organized as a particular pattern; all patterns are independent.[1] As shown in Figure 2, all actualities are free from any interaction since all actualities are whole. All objects are included in all actualities in different patterns or organizational relations. There will be many patterns that can represent the system or the reality. The representation is an object-dependent, or thus language-dependent, description of the patterns (principle) of the reality, and is not a description of the reality itself. What is represented is the function of the system.

It becomes paradoxical that the systems may be represented by their parts in different patterns, but the system does not have any properties that can be based on these parts. This is also true in the scientific system, where the parts are only used to construct the patterns represented in a theory.[2] The theory is the driving force to build a pattern according to the principle, to support the function of the system.

---

[1] Mathematically, there actualities are orthogonal to each other.

[2] For example, we do not invoke the properties of hydrogen and oxygen in our description of water.

The objects are by convention only

An object represents a basic unit used in our communication of a pattern. We accept the objects as our "building blocks of social reality."[1] The objects are our "constitutional facts" that we can use to construct the patterns that can represent reality.

In our model discussion, it will be useful to use the concept of domain. Each system has a whole domain. For convenience, we subdivide this whole domain into many sub-domains and represent each sub-domain by an object or a group of objects. That is, we may choose any group of objects to represent a system as long as the group can cover the whole domain of the system. Therefore, the group of objects is chosen as a convenient means to cover the whole domain of the system under discussion.

These objects must be interconnected to form some patterns or subsystems that can represent the whole. In a living system, the object may be a cell, or an atom, or a body part, etc. In the logic model, an object may be the basic idea represented by words.

---

[1] John R. Searle, "The Construction of Social Reality," The Free Press, 1995

Subsystems and Patterns

In general, in systems thinking, the system is represented by many interrelated subsystems or patterns. As shown in Figure 2, each subsystem consists of a subset of the objects in the system. The internal interactions form the structure of the subsystem and the subsystems will interact due to the external interactions between the subsets of the objects in different subsystems. The subsystems are *intermediate, unstable,* patterns formed by the subsets of the objects in the system. These subsystems are not stable because they are still interacting with their environments. We may view the system as a complex of subsystems. The objects in a subsystem are strongly interconnected inside the subsystem and weakly connected to the objects in other subsystems. The subsystems and their environments maintain a dynamic balance.

Each subsystem only consists of a partial set of the objects in the system, so they are only parts of the whole. Although these parts may have overlapping objects, each part shows a different pattern. These patterns cannot represent the whole reality. When the subsystems and their environments are considered together, they constitute the wholeness of the system.

Reality, System, and Actuality

In our investigation of reality, we consider the evolution of the subsystems as the process to seek reality. We are interested in the final subsystems that can represent reality. The reality is the whole system, or the system is the reality in our discussion.

As shown in Figure 2, the subsystems will interact via feedback interactions and become the final subsystems when all objects are included and all interactions are harmonized. Harmonization means that the external interactions disappear. Then the final subsystems are independent and may represent reality. In a final subsystem, all objects of the system are harmonized and organized into a particular pattern to support reality.

Therefore, each final subsystem is a particular pattern of all objects of the system to represent reality. [1]

In our philosophical discussions, we are interested only in the final subsystem, so our patterns normally refer to the final subsystem, where the representation is realistic, complete, and whole. [2] In. dualism, there are two, not just one, such final representations of the system reality.

---

[1] In mathematics, these subsystems are orthogonal in the multi-dimensional space of the reality. They are the reality vectors.

[2] The intermediate subsystems are viewed as the steps in the process philosophy which will be discussed later.

Model is Object-dependent

In our model, the reality of a system can only be represented by patterns of the objects. The patterns are based on the organization of the objects.

For example, the principle of Tao philosophy may be represented in terms of many dualistic "opposite pairs," such as Wu and Yu, Yin and Yang, Black and White, etc. The resulting pattern is a complementarity of the opposite pairs (This will be discussed in Chapter 3). In this dualistic model, although the objects are different, the patterns are the same.

The final subsystems all the *actualities* in the model. Our goal is the logic to describe actualities with the objects.

Hard and Soft Systems Thinking

We may recapture the two ways to look at the logic structure shown in Figure 3. For any reality, we may use either hard or soft systems analysis.

In hard systems analysis, we assume the properties of the objects and describe the function of the system in terms of these objects. This is the *upward process* that goes from the object level to the actuality level shown in the figure. This approach is common in scientific theory, which starts from the objects to build the subsystems, and uses the subsystems to explain the function of the whole.

The interactions and the laws of interactions between the objects are implicitly built into the theoretical framework and, often the resulting patterns formed by the objects are not explicitly shown in the theory.

On the contrary, in the soft systems analysis, we identify the function of the whole to define the functions of the subsystems and treat the subsystems as networks of objects. This is a *downward process* from the system to the subsystem level in the figure. The objects are only used to show the patterns of the subsystems. The main concern is the subsystems and their feedback interactions with the environments. The objects have a very limited role in showing the function of the whole. The properties of the objects are of secondary importance.

On the surface, these two processes appear to be opposites, but our model can show that they are equivalent in principle. The meeting place is the pattern: the pattern in the hard systems approach is in the theoretical framework and the pattern in the systems approach is explicit.

In both cases, the patterns are generated by the interactions between the objects according to a principle. This principle is the Oneness of the system. This is the basic principle in our discussion of a reality or a system. Our thinking of reality at all levels must conform to the *Principle of Oneness*.

The Principle of Oneness

The function of the system is to retain Oneness. This function must be preserved in all levels of our discussions of the structure shown in Figure 2.

In the example of the dualism of Chapter 3, we start with the two opposite objects to cover the whole domain. The objects are not sufficient to describe a reality since the objects are only parts and the reality is a whole. At the object level, all objects are interconnected properly by their interactions that follow a principle to preserve Oneness at the level. The principle is that the final subsystems will be independent of each other after the interaction are harmonized according to the principle.

We may skip the intermediate subsystems level in our discussion of the principle of Oneness since, at this level, the subsystems behave exactly like the objects at the object level and interact via the feedback interactions. We may have many levels of subsystems. The subsystems are not whole, but they are interconnected via their feedback interactions. Therefore, the intermediate subsystems at each level also preserve Oneness.

At the actuality level, we have the actualities that have the final patterns of the objects by harmonizing all interactions. Oneness is preserved in each of the actualities. In dualism, we have two independent patterns at the actuality level that can represent reality. The two actualities will have different patterns but are *simultaneous* and *equivalent* representations of the same reality. The two actualities are equivalent and are intrinsically related; therefore, the reality is not divided at the actuality level. This is how Oneness is preserved at the actuality level.

Oneness and Wholeness

The system is One and all descriptions of realities must be whole.

Oneness can only be described by negative statements, such as empty of objects, indefinite, infinite, without forms and image, etc. Our language and thinking are based on our senses of the multitudes of things in the world. These senses are represented by the objects, but we believe that the myriad things are linked to the Oneness of all. The reality is that all things are One and everything we see should reflect everything else. Everything should reflect the wholeness of the myriad things.

Therefore, the best we can do is to reconstruct the wholeness of everything. Then the reality can be represented as the wholeness of everything in everything. Each thing can show itself in a pattern that also reflects everything else. In this case, everything as a whole can be a representation of reality. In systems thinking, everything becomes an independent pattern of all the things in the world.[1]

We shall see that our actualities will have wholeness and may be reconstructed from the objects. Each actuality represents an object in a pattern that also reflects all other objects. In our logic model, the objects are our language. We may use language logically to describe the actuality that can represent reality.

Linguistic Expression of Wholeness

We shall use our language as objects to describe the patterns of actualities as reality. We assume an object represents a *simple concept* that can be expressed directly in our language.

---

[1] Everything becomes a monad with qualities specified by Leibniz's *Monadologie*. They are eternal, indecomposable, individual, subject to their own laws, un-interacting, and each reflecting the entire universe in a pre-established harmony.

However, in dualism, each actuality is a complex of two *superimposed* objects. The opposite concepts (objects) in actuality cannot be expressed directly in our language, due to the dualistic nature of our language. Therefore, an actuality remains a *complex concept* in our mind that will show interferences within the actuality when expressed in language.

As we shall discuss in Chapter 3, when we render the actuality into language, the expression will appear fuzzy, self-contradictory, and indeterminate. However, such fuzzy, self-contradictory, and indeterminate statements are the proper way to describe the nature of reality.

This is an important conclusion. Our descriptions of Oneness and wholeness are obscure because we always think in terms of objects and take objects to be real. We have to overcome our habit of dualistic thinking. For this purpose, systems thinking becomes important. General systems thinking implicitly assumes wholeness by describing the systems and the subsystems.

A General Principle

We first discovered the Principle of Oneness in the analysis of Tao philosophy. This principle shows how the function of a whole can be expressed as organizational patterns of the parts.

This principle is also recognized as systems thinking by Capra and Luisi. Their view is stated as:

> The ancient Chinese philosophers believed that the ultimate reality, which underlies and unifies the multiple phenomena we observe, is intrinsically dynamic. They called it Tao - the way, or process, of the universe. For the Taoist sages all things, whether animate or inanimate, were embedded in the continuous flow and change of the Tao. The belief that everything in the universe is imbued with life has also been characteristic of indigenous spiritual traditions throughout the ages. In monotheistic religions, by contrast, the origin of life is associated with a divine creator. (page 1)

The concept of Oneness is also the core of early Greek philosophy, Indian philosophy, and Buddhist philosophy. The same principle is also observed by most modern philosophers and scientific investigations.

The logic structure behind systems theories can be traced back to ancient Chinese, Greek, and Indian philosophy. Some examples of ancient philosophy will be in Chapter 4.

Summary of this Book

Chapter 1 Introduction is an overview of systems thinking and the underlying principle. Chapter 2 is the general systems theory and introduction to a dualistic model. Chapter 3 develops the logic structure and its applications. There are many interesting logical consequences of the model, including its relationship to Aristotle's Square of Oppositions.

Chapter 4 shows some Unusual Logical Consequences. Chapter 5 extends the logic model to the proper relationships among the past, present, and future. Chapter 6 describes systems thinking in ancient Western and Eastern philosophy. This includes systems thinking worded by Laozi, Parmenides, and the Buddha. Chapter 7 is a summary.

Appendix A is the Square of Oppositions. Appendix B is the interpretation of the Zeno Paradoxes. Appendix C lists the major keywords.

Chapter 2
General Systems Theory

If one must use metaphorical language, then let the metaphor be this: the mind and the world jointly make up the mind and the world.

Hilary Putnam
Reason, Truth, and History

In this chapter, we shall give an overall summary of the general systems theory. The earliest model is proposed as the General Systems Theory of Bertalanffy and the Science of Structure (Tektology) of Bogdanov. Systems thinking is a useful complement to the scientific analysis of a system. It has added invaluable light to our interpretation of the logic of the *Tao Te Ching*. There is a common ground in all systems analyses.

The common criterion for a living system is that it must be an integrated whole so it can be independent and exist by itself. A system consists of parts, but the properties of the system are properties of the whole, which are different from the properties of its parts. In general systems studies, the systems are almost whole with some residual interconnections and are represented as *networks* of the identified parts.

The organizing relations of the parts give rise to the properties of the system. However, the properties of the system vanish when a system is disintegrated into isolated parts. Systems study does not deal with individual objects.

It is clear that the "cause and effect" is not based on objects, but is driven by system changes. Systems thinking is trying to avoid such a "liner process" based on objects.

In general, a system is viewed as a complex of subsystems with many levels of complexity. The patterns at each level have a similar structure, consisting of the same objects (see Figure 3). For dualistic objects, there are always two equivalent subsystems. Systems thinking allows us to shift our views between these subsystems levels, without changing the basic principle at different systems levels.[1]

The properties of a particular subsystem emerge from the organization of the parts. The similarity of patterns at all levels reflects the same principle as the driving forces.

The formation of all subsystems seems to obey a principle similar to the principle of Oneness. This fact draws our attention to systems thinking. We may perceive this principle of integration as the Oneness of the system.

---

[1] This is like a fractal phenomenon. In Tao philosophy, the final destination is always the ultimate actuality. There are always ways to achieve the final actualities.

Like reality, the wholeness of the system allows it to sustain itself forever. All living systems try to preserve their wholeness or Oneness to be living. However, all living systems have not yet reached wholeness, still with some residual interconnections.[1]

The bounds of a living system are similar to the bounds of reality. A reality and a system are whole so they can last. We have investigated the nature of reality in the logic of Tao philosophy (see Reference). It is interesting to see how logic appears with systems thinking.

Historical Background

The systems have the common goal to explain the complex living systems in terms of their dynamic networks of interactions between the subsystems.

Ludwig von Bertalanffy (1901-1972), an Austrian biologist, is often credited as the pioneer of systems theory. However, Alexander Bogdanov (1873-1928), a Russian medical researcher, philosopher, and economist, had previously formulated a comprehensive theoretical framework describing the principles of organization of living systems.

---

[1] If all living systems include "death" as their elements, then they are living and have reached wholeness. We shall ignore the difference of living systems and reality in our discussions.

Bertalanffy's theory is known as the *General Systems Theory* and Bogdanov's s theory is known as *Tektology* or "the science of structures." Both try to clarify and generalize the principles of organization of all living structures. Tektology is the first attempt to arrive at a systematic formulation of the principles of organization.

Systems thinking has impacts on many fields, such as Gestalt psychotherapy, Cybernetics, catastrophe theory, chaos theory, sociology, and complexity theory, etc. Systems thinking is used in many studies of the relations of the parts and wholes, their boundaries, and interactions. Stanisław Leśniewski (1927) introduced "mereology" as the study of the whole and the parts.

Characteristics of Systems

A living system has a function to survive as a whole. In systems thinking, we assign this function to the system and the purpose of all subsystems is to preserve this function. Therefore, a system and its subsystems have a common purpose.

Systems theory is a tool to recognize the organization of the parts and their relations in the whole. The system is a whole and the subsystems are the parts. The subsystems interact with their environments and support the functions of the system. Although the subsystems are patterns of objects, systems theory usually does not describe the properties of the objects.

A living system is recognized by its unique property to survive, which is equivalent to its attempt to remain as a whole. The whole itself often remains indescribable except as a function or principle. However, the phenomena of the whole can be shown in the *patterns* or structures of the subsystems that support the function of the system. The patterns may be shown to consist of objects, but these objects themselves do not have the properties to describe the whole. The objects are networked in certain ways to represent the functions of the system.

Similarly, in philosophy, the reality is a self-sustaining system. Reality is a system of concepts. Our *conceptual* description of reality consists of many interconnected networks of concepts; each concept in turn is a complex concept of sub-concepts. The unique properties of reality are also its attempt to survive as a whole. Investigation of reality is known as *ontology*, the science of being, or the science of what-is.

There is a shared foundation for both systems theory and *ontology*. There is a common set of laws of organization. Our purpose is to establish a common logic model applicable to systems theory and ontology. The benefit is both ways. We can learn from the systems theory and also from the study of reality.

Systems Theory and Logic Model

Systems theories deal mainly with subsystems. In general, the subsystems view will have many levels of subsystems, as shown in Figure 4(a).

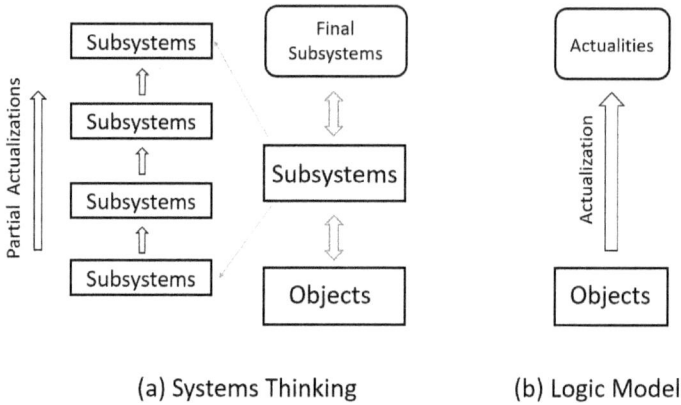

(a) Systems Thinking   (b) Logic Model

Figure 4 Systems Theory and Logic Model

Each level of the subsystem is a partial actualization of the objects into particular patterns based on the purpose of the system. These patterns may evolve and reach a dynamic balance with the environments. Each subsystem and its environment (with feedbacks) constitute wholeness at the level.

Such systems thinking is similar to the process philosophy of Whitehead or the process of Plotinus, going from the objects to the whole system. Each subsystem is subject to the constraint of wholeness or Oneness at its level.

The logic model is also subject to the constraint of Oneness. It has been successfully applied to the analysis of Tao philosophy. We have shown how language can be used to describe reality. We have identified the objects as our language and the actualities as our ultimate representations of reality.

The logic model describes the relationship between the objects and the actualities. This is shown in Figure 4(b). The logic model is concerned with how the objects can represent the actualities.

The principle is the same Oneness of reality at the object and actuality levels. In systems theories, the same principle is used in the partial actualizations of the subsystems at every level. Therefore, the logic of describing the full actualization process is the same as that for all partial actualizations of a living system. The subsystems reflect different aspects of reality.

At each level, the reality is maintained by a group of subsystems and their environments. A subsystem is a pattern formed by subsets of objects in the process of actualization. The subsystems will further integrate to form the final subsystems that can represent fully the reality. There are multiple final subsystems. Reality is represented by multiple integrated *wholes,* rather than a single pattern of all parts.

In both ways of thinking, the language is correlated to form patterns of statements, which are further integrated to form the representations of reality. Our description of reality is language-dependent. Therefore, our language shapes our view of the world.

The Patterns

In systems thinking, a system is linked to the networked patterns of the objects and not to the objects. The network is characterized by the function of the system and the complex interconnected subsystems that reflect the purpose of the system. We have two ways to study the patterns:

- In science, the properties of the whole complexity are understood by assuming the objects that cover the whole domain and by analyzing the *interactions between the objects*. The interactions give rise to *implicit patterns* that can represent the properties of the system. The patterns are represented by the objects, the interactions, and the theoretical framework. These patterns are bound by a scientific principle.

- In systems thinking, the essential properties of the system are the properties of the whole, which none of its parts have. The properties are reflected in the subsystems and their environments. The subsystems are explicit *patterns of the objects*. The analysis terminates at the patterns level.

These two approaches are equivalent if we recognize that the interactions between the objects determine the patterns and the patterns require the interactions to form. There is essentially no difference *in principle* between the two approaches.

In systems theory, the properties of the whole dictate the properties of the subsystems, and the subsystems are represented by the patterns of the objects. The subsystems interact with their environment in the same manner as the objects interact with other objects. The driving forces serve the same purpose of the system to retain Oneness. This is essentially the principle of Oneness in our logic model.

Examples of Systems Views

There are many familiar examples of systems views. For example, a table should be linked to the solid form of the atoms. If we do not recognize the networked patterns of atoms in a table, then we may think the table is mostly void. The obvious mistake is to consider the atoms and the void as real and neglect the patterns of the atoms.

Music is another simple example of systems thinking. A symphony cannot be appreciated by recognizing the notes and instruments only; the symphony is the proper arrangement of the patterns of the musical notes.

When we do not maintain the views of the system and take the objects as reality, we encounter the famous Zeno's paradoxes, which we discuss in the Appendix.

Objects and Subsystems

We think in terms of objects, but these individual objects are not real so they have to be logically correlated. We show two subsystems in Figure 5, where each subsystem consists of a subset of the objects in the system.

Within each subsystem, the objects form a pattern by *internal interactions*. The objects between the subsystems also interact with their *external interactions*. The external interactions constitute the environments of the subsystems. At the object level, the system is formed by *a complete set* of objects and their interactions. Form the patterns in a subsystem are determined by their internal interactions.

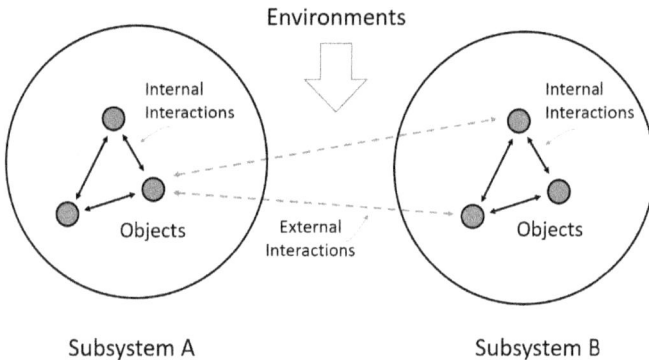

Figure 5 Subsystems and Environments

There are interactions between the subsystems due to the external interactions of the two sets of objects that are treated as the environments of the subsystems.

Subsystems and Actualities

The traditional systems and our systems thinking may be shown in Figure 6. In the traditional systems (a), each subsystem is not a complete set of objects in the system. But all subsystems together and their interactions with the environment can represent the whole system. A system generally has many subsets of objects in many subsystems with various complexities.

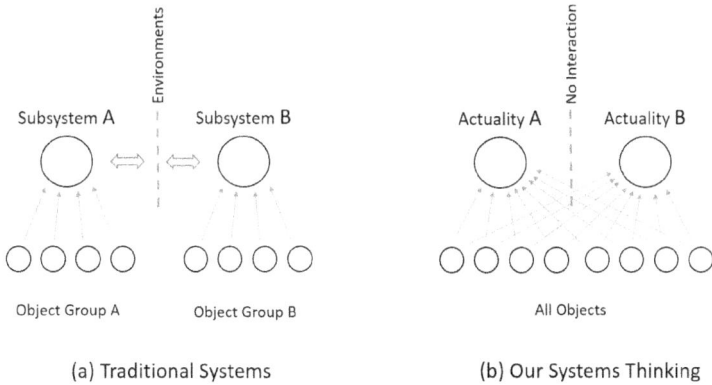

Figure 6 Subsystems and Actualities

In our systems thinking of the logic model (b), all objects participate in the formation of all actualities. All objects are formed as different patterns and each pattern represents a final subsystem. There is no environment between the actualities. All actualities are truly independent of each other. Each actuality represents the same reality or system.

Subsystems and Subsystem-domains

A subsystem has an internal structure consisting of a set of objects. The subsystem domain is the sum of the domains assigned to the objects. A subsystem is already living with its environment in a living system. We distinguish a subsystem and subsystem domain in Figure 7.

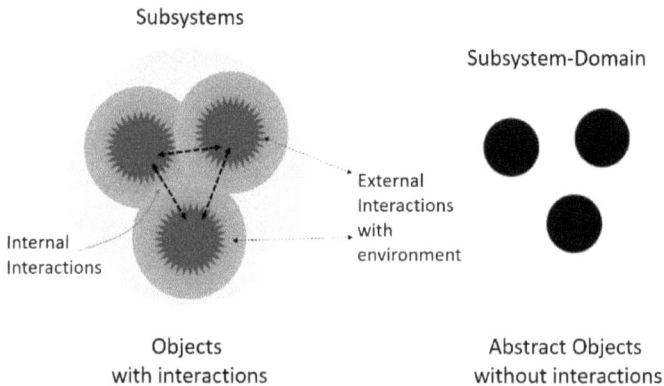

Figure 7 Parts or Subsystems and Objects

In this example, the subsystem has three objects and may have an apparent boundary identified with the objects. The objects have *internal interactions* with other objects inside the subsystem and also *external interactions* with objects outside the subsystem. The external interactions are the interactions with the environment. The structure of the subsystem is mostly determined by internal interactions. The subsystem is living by including the external interactions.

A subsystem domain is an abstract entity that covers only a sub-domains of the objects. In general systems theory, each subsystem involves a definite set of objects so subsystems have separate and non-overlapping domains. In our model, an object may appear as a member of multiple subsystems so the subsystem domains may overlap.

Network Evolution

A system is independent, but a living system generally interacts with its environment so it is not independent. In this sense, a living system evolves as a subsystem of a larger system.

A system consists of a set of subsystems with their environments. Systems thinking then deals with the evolution of these subsystems. The subsystems evolve by responding to changing environments through internal and external interactions.

The ultimate evolution of the system is to integrate all interactions of all objects in the system. In this case, all final subsystems will contain all objects and each final subsystem is a different pattern consisting of the same objects. In Figure 3, we have called these final subsystems the actualities.

A Simple Dualistic System

We shall use a dualistic system as an illustration, where we have a pair of opposite objects, to discuss the systems thinking. The opposite objects are a convenient pair to cover the whole domain of a system.

In the Hard systems view, the building blocks are the objects. By convention, we label these two objects as "opposites." It might be more appropriate to label them as "*complements*" since they complement each other to represent a whole.

The only criterion for selecting objects is that the objects must cover the whole domain of the system. Therefore, we may have many choices of different objects to represent a system. With different groups of objects, the internal structure produced by their relationship may be different, but the properties of the system remain the same. In other words, a system may be represented in many different ways with different kinds of objects. The patterns are determined by the function of the system, which maintained by the interactions between the objects.

The two objects must have interactions to hold the two objects interconnected to form the patterns of some complexity. When these interactions are partially integrated, the patterns are the subsystems. Full integration will form the actualities that can represent the whole system.   This is shown in Figure 8.

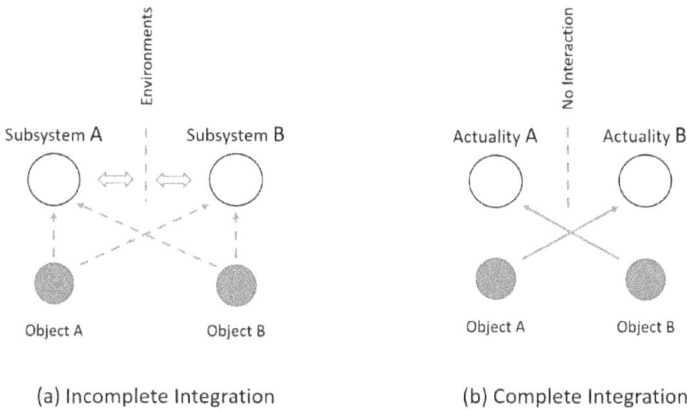

(a) Incomplete Integration   (b) Complete Integration

Figure 8 Incomplete Integration

When the interactions of the objects are not completely integrated (or harmonized), the two subsystems formed will not be independent and there are always inter-subsystem interactions.

The subsystems are *open systems* because they have interactions with external entities. This is shown in (a). In systems thinking, these residual interactions are the environments of the subsystem. The environments are required to maintain the wholeness of the system.

In a fully integrated system, the interactions between the objects are completely harmonized. The two objects form two actualities for the system. With full integration, there is no residual interaction between the actualities. The actualities are *closed systems*. This is shown in (b). In philosophy, representations for reality must have wholeness. Therefore, the actualities must be fully integrated subsystems that can reflect the characteristics of the system.

Structure of Patterns

In the systems view, the basic characteristics of a living system are shown by the patterns of the subsystems. The subsystems are interconnected because they are all open systems.

The structure of subsystems is shown in Figure 7(a) where there are always environments. In a dualistic system, a subsystem is a pattern with two objects. When the integration is incomplete, the two subsystems are still interconnected with residual interactions. The two patterns are not independent because they do not have the proper structures to be independent.[1] The structure depends on the objects and their interactions.

---

[1] In mathematics, the two subsystems are not orthogonal to each other.

The description of the system is abstract in terms of the patterns of the objects. Such description *does not* identify the properties of the objects.[1] Each object does not have an independent meaning, without referring to the meanings of other objects in the system and we may choose many kinds of objects to represent a system.[2]

In systems thinking, the structures and function of the patterns are the essences of study. For any system, the patterns are determined by the purpose of the system. The system and its subsystems of various complexities normally show a consistent pattern formed under a common principle. In systems thinking, this is called *Autopoiesis* (Self-making). This reflects Oneness as the driving teleological force for the growth of the system.

---

[1] For example, water and ice have the same objects, but their structures of patterns are different because they have different environments.

[2] For example, we may have different rules of games for baseball, tennis, basketball in order to show the meaning of *fairness* in the system. A system can be embodied in different manners by many different kinds of objects.

Structured Relationship

As shown in Figure 7(a), the two objects are partially integrated into two subsystems. Some residual interactions between the objects appear as the environments. These subsystems will further evolve by integrating more residual interactions until they become the two final subsystems. These final subsystems are the true representations of the system. All interactions between the objects are integrated so the final subsystems are free of any interaction. They are whole and independent.

A living system is between the objects and the final subsystems. It is an open system complex of partially integrated subsystems. These subsystems are submerged in their environments. We may also view these subsystems as interdependent living subsystems if these subsystems are viewed together with their environments and preserve the properties of the system.

The subsystem patterns are direct results of the interactions between the objects. In the Hard systems view, the interactions produce the patterns; in the systems view, the patterns are produced by the interaction. Therefore, patterns and interactions are equivalent.

In our logic model, we can bypass the complexity of subsystems and directly deal with the final subsystems. They are representations of reality, as shown in Figure 7(b).

A Teleological Force

There is a hierarchy of systems complexity, but all subsystems operate with the same principle, which is set by the system and is sustained throughout the system's growth.

In each subsystem, the organizations of the objects are according to a principle to support the function of the system. The interactions between the objects also ensure that the object level preserves the same principle. The environments between the subsystems ensure that subsystems are bound by the same principle. Since the same principle applies equally to different levels, we can shift between the levels without external efforts. All levels are equally true.

Each subsystem shows somewhat autonomy explicitly, but all subsystems are interconnected, so life is not localized in any subsystem. The function of each subsystem is to preserve itself and to participate in the transformation of all other subsystems. The principal acts as a teleological force.

Since a subsystem is related to all other subsystems, any change in any subsystem will have an impact on all other subsystems. Therefore, all subsystems and their environments change simultaneously to preserve the system as a whole. The change is a non-local effect.

Philosophical Reality as a System

An idealized philosophical reality may be considered as a closed system, which is independent and free from its environment. Reality must be whole so it can survive forever. Such a system must have the properties of Oneness. To describe such a system, we have to have objects that can cover the domain of reality.

A convenient way to cover the whole domain which is infinite is to use two opposite (complementary) objects A and B where $A + B = 1$. As shown in Figure 7(b), when the interactions between these two objects are fully harmonized, they will form two actualities.

In systems thinking, the two actualities are two patterns that can represent the essence of reality. The reality can only be described as Oneness which is structure-less. The actualities have wholeness with the structure of objects and can last forever as reality does.

In our logic model, we deal only with the objects and the actualities since the subsystems are only intermediate steps of representing reality.

- In Hard systems thinking, reality may be represented by the objects and their interactions. The interactions between the objects result in patterns of objects that can represent reality. Objects and their interactions are treated as though they were real in a mechanical theory. This is a common approach adopted in the analysis of philosophy.

- In systems thinking, this view is shifted. The reality is first identified and its manifestations are required to represent the same reality. We then show the manifestations in terms of the patterns of a set of objects that covers the domain of reality. The properties of the objects are not the prime essence of reality.

In systems thinking, an object becomes merely an abstract participant in a pattern to show reality. Reality cannot be associated with the properties of its objects. Only the patterns are real. The intrinsic properties of the objects disappear in the patterns.

On the surface, Hard systems thinking is very different. The properties of the Hard system's objects also become secondary when a theory is applied. The physical phenomena become the patterns of reality.

Realism and Idealism

We may view Hard systems thinking and systems thinking as traditional materialism/realism and idealism approaches, respectively, in philosophy. Realism takes objects as real; idealism takes something higher than objects as real.

We may put the two ways of thinking into one consistent framework, as our logic model, which has been applied to analyze Tao philosophy. Many interpretations of the *Tao Te Ching* can also be more conveniently expressed in systems thinking. This logic model is also consistent with the logic in systems thinking.

Process Philosophy

A system consists of the objects and subsystems, with their interactions in *dynamic equilibrium*. Systems dynamics involve a process where the objects form the subsystems and the subsystems form the final subsystem. There are many levels of the subsystems.

The process from the objects to the actualities is called *actualization* or *integration*. At any moment, we may view the whole system as a complex of subsystems at various stages of actualization. The complete actualization process is essentially the process proposed by Whitehead (1978).[1] This multi-step process may be shown in Figure 9.

---

[1] For those who are familiar with sciences, the process is essentially the same as the perturbation theory where perturbations are harmonized through a series of stages.

Here we illustrate the actualization process with three stages of integration from objects to the final integration. In each step, some residual interactions are harmonized. When the subsystems are well described, they are *objectified* to become the objects for the next stage of integration. The new objects will then interact with new residual interactions to form new subsystems. In general, there are many integration stages within the subsystems level.

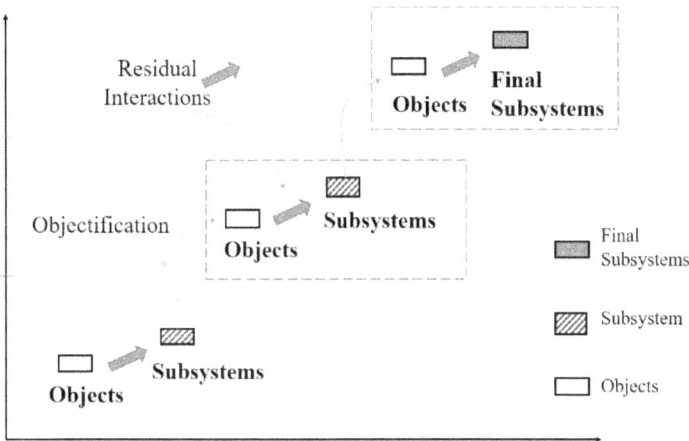

Figure 9 Multi-level Process Philosophy

Each step is a process of integration where a subsystem evolves into another subsystem with some input from its environment. In all steps, the organizations of objects may change, but the integration principle remains the same. The subsystems may change internally and externally by adjusting themselves to the environments.

In a dualistic system, the two objects will finally form two actualities that can represent reality *in the phenomenal world*. The actualities are independent and without any interaction. They can exist by themselves.

The driving force for the entire actualization process is to maintain the Oneness of the system at every step. This is the driving force for survival. The final subsystems are the ultimate states of the system we can view in the phenomenal world transcendentally. The final subsystems may disappear and merge back into Oneness, which is un-manifested.[1]

This *actualization process* is reversible. We may start with the actualities at the highest level and start to articulate the system with objects. We may say that the actualization process is a Hard system and the *articulation process* is systems thinking.

---

[1] When Oneness is manifested holistically, Laozi calls it God and Spirit. Oneness is not nothingness.

In dualism, the basic pattern when fully integrated is the *complementarity* of the objects. Each pattern covers the whole domain. The intermediate subsystems have residual interactions because of incomplete integration. All subsystems at any step have the same pattern of complementarity. *Complementarity* is universal and shows the principle of a dualistic system.

Hierarchies of integration

Since the early days of organismic biology, these multileveled structures of systems within systems have been called hierarchies of nature. According to the systems view, the essential properties of an organism, or living system, are properties of the whole.

If we "divide" the whole into its "parts," each part will also observe the properties of the whole. In our example, two final subsystems can equally represent the whole. Therefore, the two parts (final systems) are not two parts. It is similar to the holographic effects that two parts can each shows the same whole.

Although we can discern individual subsystems in any system, these subsystems are not isolated. In our model, the subsystems are interacting with each other at the subsystem level in the same way as the objects interacting with each other at the object level. Both the subsystems and the objects interact the same way and result in the same pattern of complementarity.

In the systems approach, the properties of the individual objects are not relevant since they are all relative to each other. Only the patterns of the objects have meanings and can represent the properties of the whole.

In general, a complete system consists of many heterogeneous subsystems with different levels of complexity. All subsystems emerge as the patterns of objects and appear autonomous in their environment.

The multi-level process represents a hierarchy where more and more residual interactions are harmonized at each intermediate level. The actualization at each stage *internalizes* some of the residual interaction to form intermediate subsystems.

The Final Integration

In our logic model, when all subsystems are fully integrated, the final step of integration will produce multiple co-existing final subsystems. Each final subsystem contains all objects in the system in a particular organization. Each final subsystem can represent the whole system. Therefore, the final integration does not bring all back to a single *one* representation of reality. There are always multiple representations. In the phenomenal world, dualistic thinking will produce dual realities.

We may view these fully actualized subsystems as the "monads" of the world. There are many monads in the world. All monads are in a pre-determined harmony by God, as proposed by Leibniz.[1] We can see the whole world in a grain of sand.

Integration of a Subsystem

A subsystem and its environments constitute a whole so a subsystem evolves with its environments. A subsystem may grow by including more and more interactions and more and more objects into the subsystem. We may show the growth process in Figure 10.

Here the Subsystem A grows into Subsystem B and grows into Subsystem C. As we have stated earlier, the interactions of an object could be classified as internal and external interactions. The internal interactions integrate the objects within the subsystem and the external interactions of all objects in the subsystem interact with the objects outside the subsystem.

---

[1] The principles of Leibniz's logic may be reduced to two: (1) All our ideas are compounded from a very small number of simple ideas, which form the alphabet of human thought. (2) Complex ideas proceed from these simple ideas by a uniform and symmetrical combination, analogous to arithmetical multiplication.

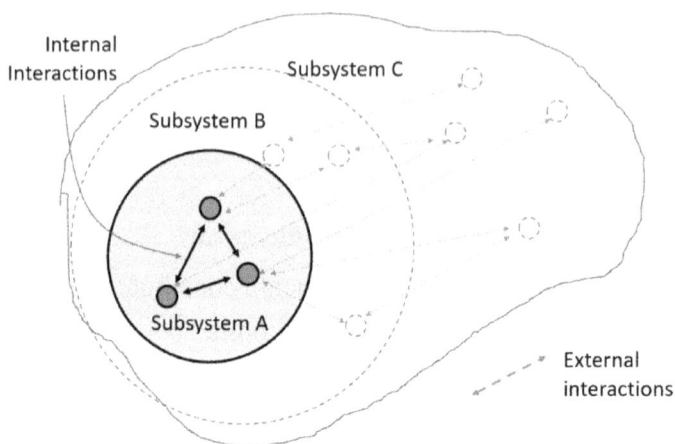

Figure 10 Subsystem Growth

Figure 10 shows the integration process of Subsystem A into B by including explicitly the interactions with three more objects outside A. By such inclusion, Subsystem A becomes B which has six objects. The subsystem changes and the environment also changes. Subsystem B then grows into C by including more objects outside B.

In this process, the subsystem grows by integrating more and more interactions. In so doing, the subsystems will include more and more objects until it contains all objects in the system. Such interactions may alter the structural patterns of the subsystem or the nature of the objects inside the subsystem.

This process of integration is traditionally depicted in Figure 11. Here an old subsystem interacts with its environment and some input from this environment transforms the subsystem and some other inputs generate the new environment for the new subsystem.

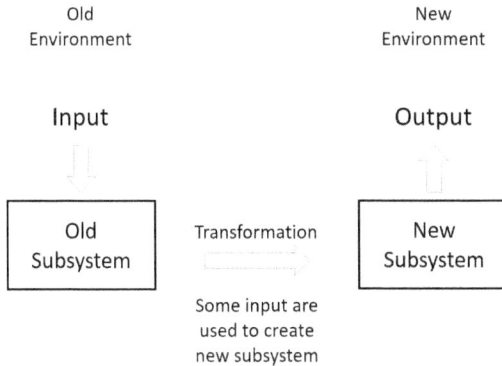

Old
Environment

New
Environment

Input

Output

Old
Subsystem

Transformation

New
Subsystem

Some input are
used to create
new subsystem

Figure 11   Integration Process

When all external interactions are fully integrated into the subsystem, the subsystems become the final subsystems, which are free and independent. In systems thinking, all objects of the system are inside the final subsystem and assume a pattern that can represent the whole, where all objects are interconnected.

Here we should note a very important consequence of integration. The final subsystem contains all objects of the system, but *there are still multiple final subsystems.* Each final subsystem is a particular *pattern* of all objects of the system. *All patterns are independent and equivalent representations of the same system.*

The Principle of Integration

All processes in a system seem to be governed only by a single principle: The driving force for a living system is its survival as a whole. This is also the purpose of reality. Therefore, we may identify reality as a complete system and consider Oneness as the principle of integration behind system and reality.

Both reality and systems have self-preservation as their common purpose. They can sustain themselves because they are whole and independent. They can be shown to obey the principle of Oneness.

Chapter 3
Logic in Systems Thinking

Looked at from anywhere, the world is full of insecurities and contradictions; looked at from Nowhere, it is a changeless, uniform whole."

Arthur Waley
The Way and Its Power

Proceed thus: if you say "The Good, add nothing in your thought: for if you add something, you will diminish it by as much as you add."

Plotinus (204 -270 CE)

In this chapter, we shall discuss the basic logic structure that can maintain the wholeness of a system. The logic is applicable to a living system and a philosophical reality.

The key to systems thinking is the preservation of the wholeness of a system. This is similar to the principle of Oneness associated with the logic of Tao philosophy.

The logic of Tao philosophy is also a form of systems thinking. The motto of systems thinking is that a system or a reality will do what it has to survive. A system will thus strive for wholeness which is stable and independent. A living system is a self-formed subject to the same logic which we have imposed on our thinking of the nature of reality. Reality is a living system.

Our model uses the language of "science" to discuss the logic in systems thinking. The scientific model will be very helpful for those who are versed in the sciences. It also allows some extrapolations that can resolve many paradoxical statements we have found in Tao philosophy.

The Logic Principle

Logic is an expression of a principle. A living system is organized according to a principle and its properties to support that principle. The logic for organizing a system and for expressing a reality follow the same principle. We identify this principle as the principle of Oneness.

Oneness ensures that the system and reality can be maintained as a whole and everlasting. This principle will be followed in all our discussions of the system.

The logic model deals with the relationship of the parts and the whole. We subdivide the whole domain of a system into many segregated sub-domains. Each sub-domain is assigned an object. Groups of sub-domains form a subsystem. The subsystems grow to cover the whole domain and form the final subsystems. The logic is the way we can use the objects to describe the final subsystem and thus show the function of the system.

There is a principle behind the process of integration. At any stage, the system must preserve the wholeness of the system and reality cannot be divided. This is the Principle of Oneness.

In dualism, the two opposite objects are not sufficient to describe reality. We have to find the *patterns* formed by these two objects to represent reality. These patterns are the results of the interactions between the objects. Thus, the objects are always correlated by their interactions at the object level. In systems thinking, wholeness is preserved by the subsystems and their interactions with the environments. Therefore, each subsystem and its environments constitute a whole.

When all interactions are integrated, each actuality covers the whole domain and can represent reality. In dualism, there will be two actualities that are equivalent to representing reality. Since the two actualities are equivalent, the reality is not *divided* at the actuality level. The reality is represented by the two actualities, which are whole. Wholeness is the universal requirement of any reality.

The Logic Model

We may now start to describe the logic model that will show how we can describe a system or a reality logically with the complementary objects.[1]

The logic model has two parts: (1) an interaction model that describes how the two objects interact to form the patterns (the actualities) that can represent the system and (2) a linguistic model to show how we can use language to describe the patterns of the complex system.

This model was developed to interpret the principle of Tao philosophy in *The Logic of Tao Philosophy*. The model was deducted from the first chapter of the *Tao Te Ching*, but the model is applicable in a dualistic system.

---

[1] We often choose to call these two objects as *complementary* instead of *opposite* since the objects are not whole and thus are not real.

The Systems Architecture

As in any dualistic system, there are two objects. In a full integration, the system architecture may be shown in Figure 12, where two objects interact to form two actualities. We denote the two objects as w and y.[1] The two objects, after full integration, form two actualities denoted as W and Y. The whole system is denoted as S.

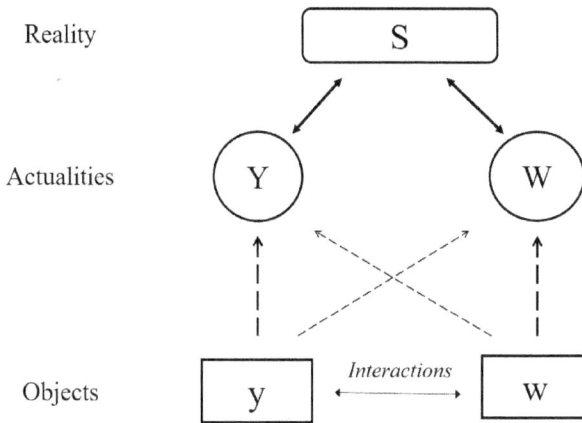

Figure 12 Systems Architecture

---

[1] We denotes the two opposite objects as w and y, after Laozi designates the two objects as Wu and Yu in the first Chapter of the *Tao Te Ching*.

In this architecture, the objects belonging to sub-domains are not whole. Therefore, these objects must be interconnected by their *interactions* at the object level so the whole object level can retain its reality.

The objects interact and form two actualities at the *actuality level*. The interactions of the objects will ensure that these actualities are whole and independent so that there is no interaction between them as shown in Figure 11. In this model, each actuality is a full representation of reality. The two actualities are equivalent since they are formed by the same objects, same interactions, and the same principle of interaction.[1]

Actualization and Articulation

In the Hard systems view, we identify first the objects and their interactions and then determine the properties of the system. This is the *actualization process* shown in Figure 11. This is the upward integration process of objects. The objects and interactions are treated as though they are real. The results of the interactions are reflected in the properties of the system. The original properties of the objects disappear and the objects form implicit patterns within the theoretical framework.

---

[1]   We may also apply this simplified model to a living system. For an example in Chinese medicine, we may identify two *abstract* organs as two objects, such as stomach and foot. At the actual level, these two abstract objects are interconnected so that they form the "actual stomach" and "actual foot," in which the "stomach" and "foot" are interconnected, so that we can find the condition of the stomach by the responses in the "actual foot" or vice versa. This is the concept of holistic healing.

In systems thinking, this process is reversed. We first identify the function of the system as the reality and then analyze the subsystems (the actualities) to support the function. We then identify the patterns of the networked objects required to represent the subsystem. The reduction stops at the patterns of the objects and we do not need to identify the properties of the objects. Such a downward process may continue to reveal the objects. This downward process is called *articulation.*

Actualization and articulation occur at the same time and are reversible. In either way, they are bound by the same principle. In systems thinking, the organizational patterns of the objects reflect the properties of the system. In Hard systems thinking, the interactions reflect the properties of the system. Therefore, the interactions determine the patterns and the patterns are implicit in the theory of interactions.

Patterns and Interactions

Patterns and interactions are equivalent ways to represent the wholeness of the system. Interactions determine the patterns and the patterns determine the interactions. The interactions and the patterns are equivalent and are the required results of the same principle. We must maintain the interactions between the objects to avoid fragmentation of the system.

Due to such interactions, the objects are mixed in the patterns. Each pattern is a relation between the two objects. The interactions ensure that the patterns in the actuality can fully exhibit the properties of the system. At the object level, the interactions are explicit but, at the actuality level, the interactions between the objects become implicit within the pattern structure.

Although our objects constitute the living systems, the objects are by themselves not alive. Whatever is alive is the *holistic* patterns of the objects in the actualities. In systems thinking, what is alive is the subsystems that are supported by the environment.

The Interaction Model

We need a logic model to describe the actuality in terms of the objects. The interactions between the objects are responsible for forming the actuality. In general, we do not know the nature of these interactions, except that the resulting actualities must be whole. Under this condition, we need an interaction model to provide the relationship between the objects and the actualities.

In the total system, the two objects are unstable because they have interactions, but the actualities are stable because the interactions are harmonized.

The Interaction Model may be shown in Figure 13. In this actualization process, the two objects, y and w, are harmonized by their interactions to form two "stable" actualities, Y and W. *"The actualities must be free from any interaction"* is the *only* condition that we have imposed on this model. The condition ensures that the actualities are independent.

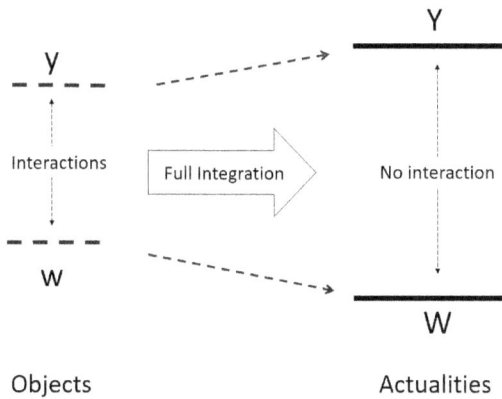

Figure 13 The Actualization Process

In this process of integration, the opposite objects are "harmonized." so it is also a "harmonization process." In the process, the objects lose their properties in the system; only the patterns are meaningful. Such an interaction model is commonly used in sciences to find stable states from unstable states through interactions.

In science, the interaction is assumed between the objects to determine the proper final states. However, in our model, we do not know the interactions. The only thing we know is that the actualities (the final subsystems) must be free and independent. This is the *only* condition that we can impose on the system. Fortunately, with this condition alone, we can solve the interaction model analytically. This condition is according to the Principle of Oneness.

This means that we do not have to know the details of the interactions to solve the problem.

Relational Structure of Patterns

This actualization process is a standard problem in science and its solution is well-known. Without showing the mathematical derivations, we may express the final states Y and W by the following equations:

$$\mathbf{Y} \ = \ a\,\mathbf{y} \ + \ b\,\mathbf{w} \qquad (1)$$
$$\mathbf{W} \ = \ a\,\mathbf{w} \ - \ b\,\mathbf{y} \qquad (2)$$

Equation 1 Relational Structure of Patterns

These equations show the patterns of the objects within each actuality. The two actualities have strict pattern configurations with objects. The participation proportions, shown as coefficients a and b, are determined by the strength of the interactions. The patterns Y and W are determined by the objects and their interactions.

The actualities are a *superposition* of the objects. The coefficients (a, b) represent the degree of participation of each object in the patterns. If the objects chosen are already close to the actualities, the interaction will be weak and the mixing will be small ($b \ll a$); if the objects chosen are far from the actualities, the interaction will be strong, and the mixing will be large ($b \sim a$) .

The mathematical results of Equation 1 are more precise than what can be expressed by ordinary language. We may interpret these equations in many ways.

The Complementarity Patterns

Equation 1 shows the general patterns of reality. We think in terms of y and w. The reality is Y and W. In dualistic thinking, these patterns ensure that the structure of Y and W preserves the wholeness of the system.

We obtained these equations in 2006 but immediately faced the proper interpretation of these simple equations to the public as the core of Tao philosophy. Only after we identified the patterns shown in Equation 1 with the familiar Tai-chi Diagram 太極圖 in Chinese philosophy, we became confident with these equations and the model. This is shown in Figure 14:

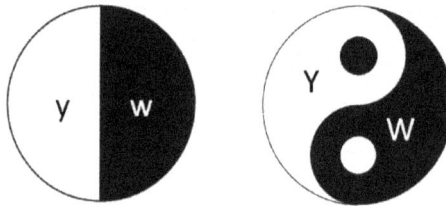

(a) Objects   (b) Patterns in System

Figure 14 Complementarity Pattern of Reality

Figure 13(a) is the traditional dualistic view, where the two objects are segregated; each object occupied a sub-domain. Figure 13(b) is just a graphic representation of the mathematical relations of Equation 1.

We may show that the ancient Tai-chi pattern is the most general pattern to represent any reality in dualistic thinking. The patterns are general and are independent of the particular objects as long as they are an opposite pair sharing the domain of the system.[1] The model has minimal assumptions and the results are most general.

The two patterns Y and W are independent and free, but they are internally interconnected because their patterns depend on the same set of coefficients. They are results of the same objects and interactions under the same principle. We can switch from one pattern to the other without any effort. The two patterns appear at the same time and are equivalent. They represent equally the properties of the same system. In ontology, the two actualities are *ontologically* equivalent.

We have deduced the results from Chapter 1 of the *Tao Te Ching*. The mathematical results were obtained by analyzing Chapter 1 alone.

---

[1] For convenience, any opposite pair can always cover the whole domain.

The Principle of Complementarity

Each actuality is a whole and the *complementarity* of the objects restores the wholeness. In dualism, there will be two realistic representations for a reality. Each representation consists of the two objects as a complementarity pattern. We recognize this as *the principle of complementarity*.

The objects may have meanings in their respective sub-domains, but these meanings cannot be used to describe fully the actuality, because two objects are *superimposed* to form patterns that can represent reality. The superposition contains the *interferences* between the objects and assumes completely different characteristics. We should also note that, as shown in Equation 1, the objects inside an actuality are incomplete (the coefficients are less than 1) so they are *concealed* or *implicit*. Furthermore, they have interference patterns that cannot be simply related to the objects. The properties of the actualities emerge from the patterns, rather than the properties of the objects.

An Illusion

If we think in terms of the opposite objects, the actualities will exhibit self-contradictory characteristics of the objects. This is only an illusion since we mistake the objects to be real and meaningful. This is a well-known *dualistic fallacy*.

Unless we can overcome the habit of Hard systems thinking in terms of objects, the concept of superposition or the interferences of objects is very difficult to clarify. Complementarity remains a difficult concept in a dualistic world because we think that objects are real. This concept of complementarity has been extensively discussed in quantum theory.

Systems Thinking

In systems thinking, we may overcome the concepts of the objects and observe the patterns of objects only. These patterns have implicit complementarity and superposition and will show the holistic nature of the system.

The systems approach has the advantage of preserving reality by suspending all dualistic judgments based on objects. We may convince ourselves to maintain the concept of wholeness and see the representations of reality directly.

The two objects are abstract, in the sense that the two objects do not *exist* and do not balance against each other inside the subsystem. In complementarity, they release each other from their characteristics as an object.[1]

---

[1] A familiar example in Chemistry may help us not to think of an actuality in terms of its objects. When we describe water, it is clear that we cannot think of hydrogen and oxygen. Water does not have any property of hydrogen and oxygen..

Modern Sciences

In sciences, the complementarity of particle and wave, or space and time, is very fundamental. Such a concept has been discussed extensively. We may treat particle and wave as objects and identify quantum theory as a new pattern of particle and wave. The same thinking may be applied to other pairs of objects, such as matter and energy, time and space, etc.

Quantum theory has adopted elaborate mathematical manipulations to show the consequences of complementarity. We have discussed the relation between quantum and Tao philosophy in a separate book, the *Dynamic Tao and Its Manifestations.*

Our appreciation of modern sciences may help in our understanding of the principle of Oneness in systems theory.

Logical Dualism and Ontological Dualism

It is convenient to distinguish two kinds of dualism so that we do not think that dualism has no truth. Both the objects and the actualities are dualistic. The objects cannot represent reality, but the actualities can. To avoid confusion on the nature of dualism, we can distinguish two kinds of dualism:

- At the object level, we have the *traditional dualism*. The dualistic objects obey the formal logic of Aristotle, such as "exclusive middle." The objects are parts and are mutually exclusive.
- At the actuality level, we have *ontological dualism*. The actualities are whole and are realities and obey a different kind of logic. The two actualities are equivalent representations of reality.

The objects are traditional dualism and the actualities are ontological dualism. Ontology is related to reality. In ontological dualism, the two actualities are equivalent and form a special dualism. Ontological dualism was part of Aristotle's Square of Opposition.

We should not take any object to be real, although they are useful in describing the actualities in terms of their formation of patterns. In the *Tao Te Ching*, Laozi has used many different pairs of objects to show the patterns of complementarity that can represent the reality of Tao.

The Principle of Equivalence

In dualism, reality may be represented by two independent patterns. Each pattern consists of two objects organized into a pattern that is a representation of reality. The two patterns co-exist at the same time and are equivalent representations of reality. In *ontological dualism*, both are true so that

The opposite of a truth is another truth.

This is the Principle of Equivalence.[1] The two truths are under the same reality. This is different from *traditional dualism,* where the opposite of a truth is an untruth. The two truths must be related by a special structure shown in Equation 1 or the Tai-chi Diagram.

The principle of equivalence owes its existence to the principle of Oneness and the Principle of Complementarity. It leads to many interesting logical consequences.

We have found this principle in many examples in Tao philosophy. This principle is very important in a multi-cultural society where the truth may be represented in many ways equally and truly. Many interesting consequences can resolve many paradoxes, as shown in Chapter4.

---

[1] The doctrine of two truths in the Buddhist philosophy, and the Pre-Socratic Parmenides can be best represented as to the equivalence of the actuality level and the actuality level. See Chapter 4.

Square of Opposition

These two kinds of dualism (traditional and ontological) are not new. The doctrine of the square of opposition originated with Aristotle in the fourth century BCE and has occurred in logic texts ever since. Our model has great similarity to the traditional square of the opposition of Aristotle.

We may identify our model as shown in Figure 11 with Aristotle's *Square of Opposition.* Although the Square has not been widely explored, it is important in our model discussion. See Appendix A for more discussions.

We may identify the objects as the *contraries* and the actualities as the *subcontraries.* The subcontraries may be both true (when they are properly configured).

The actualities are subcontrary because the actualities consist of two contraries (objects). They are equivalent because they have the structure of *complementarity* of the two objects. Not all subcontraries are equivalent.

Systems Thinking

In systems thinking, patterns are complementarities of the objects. We should avoid considering the two objects as opposites; they are just complemented as a whole. The actualities are two patterns formed by these two objects. The properties of the actuality are the properties of the patterns. The properties are the complementarity of the objects, not those of the objects. [1]

Transformation of Actualities

The actualities are free and independent. There is no interaction and no change in the laws of interaction between the actualities. [2] Transformations between the two actualities can happen spontaneously without any efforts or awareness These changes are superficial only; there is no transition or change in the essence. The principle represented in each actuality does not change. [3] Strictly speaking, there is no transition between actualities.

---

[1] A familiar example in Chemistry may help us not to think of an actuality in terms of its objects. When we describe water, it is clear that we cannot think of hydrogen and oxygen. Water does not have any property of hydrogen and oxygen. The difference between water and ice is in the patterns of the objects. See Ref.1 for geometrical representation.

[2] There is an interesting phenomenon in modern science called *spontaneous symmetry breaking*. A completely symmetric system may become two systems under influence of a field. However, the laws of interaction remain the same in each system.

[3] In such transformation, the laws of interaction do not change. Chuang-tzu 莊子 identifies this transformation as Hua 化.

The Final Patterns reflect the same Principle

The two final subsystems are the result of the same objects with the same interaction under the same principle, so they are two equivalent ways to represent the same system. This is explicitly stated by Laozi in the *Tao Te Ching*.

The relationship between the objects in the two patterns follows the same law of interactions. Therefore, we can switch from one pattern to the other without requiring any change in interaction. The two patterns are always there, we just switch our "awareness" to them.

The properties of the system are reflected equally in the two fully integrated subsystems. Each final subsystem is a structure of both objects. Both objects must appear at the same time, at all times. There is no possibility of a cyclic transition between the objects in the patterns. No object gets created or destroyed since both objects are there all the time to constitute a whole.

When we switch between the final subsystems, we may falsely sense a transition between the objects. That is an illusion since both objects are always there and the laws of interaction do not change. Switching between subsystems seems to be a flip of mind only.

Potentiality and Actuality

To use popular terminology, the objects are objects of potentiality and the actuality is a pattern of potentiality integrated into a whole.

What appears in actuality is not objects, but the potentialities of various objects. In the theory of forms, the forms are patterns of objects.

Other Forms of Representation

The mathematical relations (Equation 1) may be interpreted in many forms. This is the advantage of using such an analytical result. The model can also be related to many scientific models of nature.

For example, the relationship between the objects and the actualities may be shown in vector form or matrix form. In such representations, the objects lose the meaning of being opposite to each other. They are just the necessary complements to represent reality in vector form.

Geometry of Reality

We may view the domain of a system or reality as a multi-dimensional space. Each object is a dimension of this space. The two objects serve as the coordinates to define the space of reality. The actualities are may be represented as two-dimensional vectors in this space.

In dualism, the objects define the coordinates of the system in two-dimensional space. Then the patterns of the actualities are the *reality vectors* in that space, as shown in the following Figure:

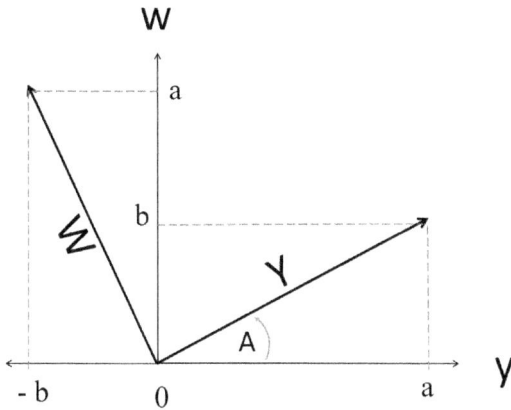

Figure 15 System Space and Reality Vectors

Here, we have two objects (w and y) as the coordinates of our system space. We may think in terms of the coordinates, but the realistic system representations are the reality vectors in this space. Systems thinking looks at the vectors directly. The classical way of thinking (based on objects) differs from the systems thinking. Angle A shows the misalignment of our classical thought with reality.

In systems thinking, the reality vectors are the targets of our pursuit. We may achieve our pursuit by modifying our classical thinking towards the reality vectors.

Geometrically, we are trying to reduce angle A by "turning" the "wheel of thought" (coordinates) gradually towards the actualities. We can think more closely with reality by adjusting our thinking coordinates towards the actualities. An "enlightenment" is reached when our thinking coincides with reality.

The Matrix Form

For mere mathematical interest, we may also express Equation 1 as a matrix relation:

$$\begin{bmatrix} Y \\ W \end{bmatrix} = \begin{bmatrix} a & b \\ -b & a \end{bmatrix} \begin{bmatrix} y \\ w \end{bmatrix}$$

Equation 2   Matrix of Transformation

where the 2x2 matrix is a rotation matrix. The coordinates, y, and w, are rotated through this matrix to form Y and W. The points with (a, b) pairs map out a trajectory moving from (y, w) to (Y, W). That is the path of integration.

The matrix ensures that our thought is aligned properly to represent reality.

Laws of Interaction and Teleology

The interactions between the objects at the object level must follow certain laws of interaction to preserve the proper order of the myriad things at the object level. Laozi calls these laws of interactions the *Te* 德. In Tao philosophy, Te is the proper way to preserve the natural order of the myriad things.

The Laws of Interactions

The laws of interactions ensure that the interactions of the objects will result in free and independent actualities. In our formulation of the logic model, the only condition we have imposed on these interactions is that the actualities must be free and independent. This is because the actualities are realities, so they must be free and whole.

With this condition alone, we can solve the interaction model mathematically and we do not have to know the details of the interaction to find the resulting patterns. The result is that the objects will form two patterns of complementarity as the actualities. The laws of interaction preserve and reflect the order of Tao.

In terms of our daily activity, we have to act according to Te and our actions will preserve the natural order.

Teleological Forces

All interactions have a single purpose. Such interactions are *teleological*.

We should also recognize that the interactions are introduced at the object level to compensate for the artificial separation of the dualistic objects. Therefore, these interactions are only as real as the objects. In other words, these interactions are not real in the whole domain. These interactions do not exist at the actuality level.

The interactions are artificial at the object level. The only purpose of these interactions is to drive all objects to form actualities that can represent reality. The laws of interaction appear whenever we are dealing with the objects in a dualistic system, from yin-yang interactions to Wu-Yu interactions. Therefore, there is a sole purpose and pattern for the interactions. The same principle applies whenever the system is not yet fully integrated.

Such teleological forces do not exist when the system is fully integrated.

Tao and Te are equivalent

In systems thinking, the function of Tao is represented as patterns of objects and Te is the laws of interaction between the objects to create the patterns.

Therefore, Te is the interactions that determine the patterns and the Tao is the patterns that demand the interactions. So Tao and Te are equivalent: Tao is the transcendental principle of the natural order. Te is the law of interactions in the phenomenal world.[1]

The Linguistic Model

Equation 1 shows the *conceptual relations* between objects and actualities. We need to express these concepts in words, that is, to quantify the concepts into words. For this reason, we introduce a *linguistic model* to express the *complex* actualities and the *simple* objects in words for our communication.

These objects are simple because they have no internal structure and maybe the basic units in our communication. The objects may be expressed directly in terms of our established language. The actualities are complexes of opposite objects and require special attention to render them in words.

---

[1] We may further identify the Te corresponding to Heng Tao 恆道 is called Heng Te 恆德 and Te corresponding to the actualities (Heng Wu and Heng Yu) is the Obscure Te 玄德.

We use the linguistic model to quantify the complex actualities in terms of our language. It will show the logic required to describe the actualities. The logic is complicated because of the interferences of the objects within the actuality. We have shown in the *Logic of Tao Philosophy*, that the linguistic description of reality is fundamentally inadequate and will necessarily be *vague, self-contradictory, and indeterminate*. However, the reality itself is always conceptually clear, non-contradictory, and determinate.

We may be able to overcome the language problem with this simple Linguistic Model. Quantum theory has a similar problem of rendering the conceptual wave function into measurable quantities. We have adopted essentially the same model to overcome the difficulties of language.

Simple and Complex Concepts

We first identify the objects as simple concepts and the actualities as complex concepts.

The objects are chosen to represent the basic units of our shared experiences that have been reduced to simple concepts and coded in our language. The actualities are complex concepts because they consist of superimposed objects. We have to reduce both simple and complex concepts into language so we can develop a logic model to describe the actuality. This is the *"quantification"* of concepts.

- Quantification of Simple Concepts - The objects are the basic units for our communication. These objects can be identified directly with the language we use for communication. Therefore the quantification of an object may be expressed as a simple word.
- Quantification of Complex Concepts – The actualities contain a complex of simple concepts. The actualities may be expressed with complex patterns of words.

We are used to thinking in terms of objects, so the opposite objects will create interference and contradictions in our minds. The objects are well-accepted concepts in our dualistic world, but the actualities are mysterious. The purpose of our linguistic model is to quantify the patterns of actualities in words and provide a framework for the necessary logic to describe the system. Quantification of the actualities is equivalent to the quantification of reality.

Quantification of Reality

The reality is shown as the actualities. To quantify these actualities, we shall borrow a simple scientific model to quantify the actualities.

In science, we use mathematical functions to describe the state of a physical phenomenon. We can quantify these mathematical functions to show the physical measurements are related to the square of the mathematical functions.[1]

The conceptual actualities are shown as mathematical functions in Equation 1 and quantification of these functions will give us a linguistic description of the actualities.

Quantification is given as the square of the functions. To simplify our notations, we represent the square of the function x by a bracketed entity [x], i.e., [x] is the quantification of the function <x>. From Equation 1, the quantifications of actualities may be written as:

$$[Y] \; = \; \{ a^2 [\, y\,] + b^2 [\, w\,] \} + a\, b\, [y^*w]$$

$$[W] = \; \{ a^2 [\, w\,] + b^2 [\, y\,]\} \; - a\, b\, [w^*y]$$

Equation 3   Characteristics of the Actualities

---

[1] For example, the electromagnetic wave is reduced the measurable electromagnetic strength, which are the square of the mathematical function. In quantum theory, the square of the wave function is related to physical measurements.

Equation 3 is the key result of our Linguistic Model. These equations represent the linguistic descriptions of the actualities or reality in terms of the language.

Here [y] and [w] represent the quantifications for the objects y and w, respectively. They can be expressed in our conventional language The cross-terms [y*w] and [w*y] represents products of the two-way interactions of the two objects y and w.

To describe the actualities, we may use (1) simple terms of conventional language associated with the objects, and (2) additional cross-terms that cannot be associated directly with the objects. The cross-terms depend on the interactions of both objects. Therefore, for the linguistic description of the actuality, we have to introduce new languages [w*y] and [y*w] in the description.

Linguistic Expression of Reality

In Equation 3, there are two distinct parts in our descriptions of the actualities. We have:

- The first part (shown within the curly brackets) can be expressed in terms of our ordinary language. This part consists of words associated with simple objects with opposite meanings. However, it is with *reduced* clarity (since a, b are less than 1). Therefore, the description of the system in terms of words will be "vague and self-contradictory."

- The second part [y*w] or [w*y] is the products of two-way interferences of the two objects. The products cannot be determined in the original world of the objects. Whenever we observe the products from any object, the other part will come into it as the result of the interactions. These cross-terms represent an "indeterminate" entity that cannot be clearly described by the objects. This term belongs to the third world, not in the original dualistic world.

The above two types of phenomena are created by the interaction interferences between the objects. We may conclude that our description of the actualities in terms of the objects will always appear to be "vague, self-contradictory and indeterminate."

Since the objects are parts, this is often expressed in systems thinking as the whole more than the sum of parts. Our analytic solution (Equation 3) gives this concept a much more precise meaning.

Two Views on Reality

Equation 3 allows two ways to view reality. These two views correspond to the systems view and the Hard systems view, or the traditional idealism and realism.

Systems View and Hard systems View

We may look at each side of Equation 3 as:

- The Left Side – It is the systems view, where the reality is revealed to us as two equivalent actualities. These actualities are whole and independent. The patterns of actuality consist of two vague objects and one indeterminate object.
- The Right Side – It is the Hard systems view, where reality is described by two vague objects and other indeterminate objects. The indeterminate objects are identified as the third object in the system.

Realism and Idealism

The logic model can also reconcile traditional realism and idealism in philosophical discussion. Realism is like the Hard systems view and idealism is the systems view. The realists take the objects to be real; the idealists take the patterns to be real. These two views are proven to be equivalent in our model.

Equation 3 shows how the actual level and the object level are equivalent. In terms of conventional terminology, the entities on the left are the ideals and the entities on the right are the realities.

- Realism - For realists, the objects are real, so the third world is real. We should note that the third world appears only at the object level. In the world of realism, there are three realistic entities.[1]
- Idealism - For idealists, the actualities are real, so the third world does not exist. In the world of idealism, there are two realistic entities

The views of idealism and realism are logically equivalent. Their differences are only superficial.

Fuzzy Logic and The Third World

We may also recognize that the logic represented by Equation 3 has some similarities to the Fuzzy Logic and the Three World Logic.

---

1 Hilary Putnam gave an example of three objects. The world of idealism will have three real entities and the world of realism will have seven real entities. (Putnam 1987, p.18). This is consistent with our model.

Fuzzy Logic

The first part in Equation 3 consists of "vague and self-contradictory" objects, a^2 [y] $+b^2$[w], which is similar to the usual fuzzy logic,[1] where the two opposite objects appear with various proportions to represent the whole ($a^2 + b^2 = 1$).

However, the second part in Equation 3 is not part of the usual fuzzy thinking. This part cannot be attributed to either one of the interacting objects. Fuzzy logic is therefore not complete in describing reality.

The Third World

The second part of Equation 3, ab[y*w] or ab[w*y], is indeterminate in terms of the original two objects. We need to treat this term as a new object. This part will become determinate when it is understood and viewed as a new object. The science philosopher Karl Popper identifies this part as the "third world" in his "three-world system."[2]

Popper cites an example of such a third world: With an artist and his canvas, a piece of artwork is a definite creation of an artist with a canvas. The artwork is the part that is neither the artist nor the blank canvas.

---

[1] Kosko, Bart, *Fuzzy Thinking: The New Science of Fuzzy Logic*, Hyperion, 1994

[2] Popper, Karl, *Three Worlds* – The Tanner Lecture on Human Values, The University of Michigan, 1978.

This third world shows that the whole is not determined only by its parts, there is always something new required. When we describe reality in terms of the existing words, there is always a new object that forces us to form a new concept and create a new term to describe the whole world. This is the result of the interactions.

This is also a natural logic of mereology,[1] where the mereological sum is larger than the sum of the parts. This is the *mereological principle* as driven by the Oneness of nature and the nature of our language. Again Equation 3 is a clear statement of this principle. We can extend this result to a system of more than two objects.

Is it a Language Problem?

The model shows that our *conventional dualistic* language is always inadequate to give a positive and definite description of reality. The description will always be vague, self-contradictory, and indeterminate. It will always demand new objects to describe the third world at the object level. The object level is the language level. Such a creative process is endless.

---

1 Mereology is the formal theory of part-whole relations.

As long as we think in terms of the existing objects, the reality cannot be fully described. Only if we can overcome the limits of our language and think in terms of the patterns, the description of reality may be achieved. As long as our language is dualistic, our ordinary language will remain inadequate at the object level.

Only if the concept of complementarity is overwhelmingly integrated into our language, our thinking habits may be able to overcome the rigidity of our language.

We may thus say that the difficulty in describing reality is like our language. But, if we can think holistically and read between the lines, the reality is there to be comprehended, without words. Words are like "fingers pointing to the moon."

Systems thinking depends on the patterns of language to make the description alive as a symbol to represent reality.

Summary of The Logic Model

This chapter prescribes the rules for the logical description of reality. The model provides a platform to steer our minds away from dualistic fallacies. We may summarize the model as:

Complementarity Patterns

In both systems thinking and Hard systems view, reality may be represented *conceptually* as patterns of complementary of the opposites. This complementarity pattern may be expressed analytically as a mathematical function. The structure of the pattern may be derived from a simple scientific model and interpreted analytically.

This pattern is the well-known Tai-chi diagram. This concept of complementarity is also widely discussed in quantum theory. From this pattern, we may under the relationship between the objects and reality.

Avoid Dualistic Fallacies

The model shows that the objects are abstract representations of well-established concepts in our dualistic language and should not be taken to be real. Once we take the objects to be meaningful and real, we are in dualistic fallacies and it is hard to recover.

It will take our mind to overcome the apparent "self-contradictory" description of reality, in the Hard systems way of thinking. The model shows a systematic way to avoid such fallacies.

Systems Thinking

Systems thinking is an important complementary way of common Hard systems thinking, which takes the objects as real. The system is bound by its function and is described by patterns of objects to support the function. The patterns of objects serve a specific function in the system. The objects are only used to show the patterns. The objects are not considered to have their reality in systems thinking.

Such systems view will avoid falling into dualistic fallacies.

Description of Reality is always Vague

As described in the model, when the reality is expressed in words, the words will be perplexing to us. However, by understanding nature, we can still sense the truth in between the words.

The description of reality will logically consist of vague and contradictory (opposite) statements to cover the whole domain of reality. The description of reality will necessarily include indeterminate statements to account for the conceptual interferences within the whole.

Interference between two objects always requires a third object to be defined. Such as the interaction between an artist and canvas produces the word "artwork."

Reality is not Vague

By definition, reality must be clear. Although the description of reality is vague, the important fact is that the reality being described is not vague. The vague, contradictory, and indeterminate words are necessary to follow a principle coherently, so the structure of the linguistic description is not arbitrary. Systems thinking is a useful way to provide an alternative view to the traditional Hard systems view based on objects.

Paradoxes are Resolved

Many paradoxes in the *Tao Te Ching* may be resolved with the logic model. We can also apply to model to the paradoxes in time (past, present, future) and the famous Zeno paradoxes. There are many unusual consequences of this logic model, many examples will be discussed in the next Chapter.

Chapter 4
Unusual Logical Consequences

In the previous chapter, we have developed a complete logic model for a dualistic system. Equation 1 is the main result of our logic model. It is the conceptual relation between the objects and the actualities. From this equation, we have derived the nature of the linguistic description of reality.

The logic model can help us see many unusual logical consequences that appear paradoxical at the first sight, but are logical. Many obscure words of Laozi may be shown to be reasonable. The perpetual Zeno paradoxes are discussed in the Appendix.

Reality and Objects

Here we review some properties of reality and objects.

Reality is Multiple

In a dualistic system, the system may be equally represented by two actualities, which have different patterns but are equivalent in representing the function of the system. The reality is *multiplied* in the phenomenal world. However, the reality is not divided since each representation is a complete and equivalent representation of the same reality. The two patterns are results of the same interactions of the same pair of objects with the same laws of interaction. Therefore, the two final subsystems must be equivalent and the system has not been divided.

For any set of objects, we have many equivalent ways to represent a world. Moreover, we may have different sets of objects, so the number of equivalent worlds is multiplied. This is the many-worlds theory.

Each set of objects may form several particular patterns and there is an infinite number of such sets. Any set of objects can independently represent the system. In each pattern, the opposite natures of the objects do not contribute to the properties of the system. Their natures have been transformed by their interactions into patterns. [1] This phenomenon will appear mysterious to us when we think in terms of objects.

In each pattern, the two objects are in complete harmony. As Heraclitus says in his fragment: "They do not understand how that which differs with itself is in agreement: harmony consists of opposing tension, like that of the bow and lyre."

Reality as Relational Patterns

Reality is not a mixture of objects. In our dualistic model, the reality is expressed as *complementary* of two opposite objects. Our model shows such a pattern of complementarity is the proper way to preserve wholeness for reality. Complementarity may be expressed as a *conceptual* relational pattern of the two abstract objects.

---

[1] We often say that the objects are harmonized. The major reason may be that the characteristics of the objects are made soft and tender by Chi. The objects are actually paired off or put together as a pair to show the pattern of the system to be represented. It may be more appropriate to say that the characteristics of the patterns are always soft and tender.

The properties of the system cannot be reflected by the properties of the objects. Each object belongs to different a sub-domain so it has no reality in the whole domain. We must include both objects in the description of a system.[1]

In other words, reality cannot be represented as a single object. A single object cannot have reality. There is no "thing-in-itself" of a thing or there is no form of a single object. The model is unlike the process of Hegel, the final integration process is not to integrate all objects into some other *unitary object*.

Superposition of Objects

Superposition is a complicated conceptual structure expressed in simple mathematical relations.   The two actualities are a *superposition of the objects*. The properties of these superimposed patterns are different from the properties of the objects. Such a pattern of superposition is complementarity and holds for any pair of opposites.

As shown in Equation 1, the objects in the superposition are not the whole objects (a, b < 1) and are interfering with each other. The structure of an actuality contains only some "parts" of all objects. The objects are entangled.

---

[1] There are many similar experiences in our daily life. For example, we cannot describe a chicken without mentioning egg, since chicken and egg constitute a pattern.

The reality must have both objects in superposition. We cannot perfect an object and make it a reality (a thing-in-itself). An object cannot become a reality by itself. There is no reality behind a single object. Dual objects must harmonize each other to form dual "different but equivalent" representations of reality.

Change of any object entails a change of all other objects to preserve the system as a whole. Any local change will cause global evolution. This is a *nonlocal* phenomenon.

Superposition will disappear in our mind only when we can think directly with actualities, i.e., with the reality vectors shown in Figure 4.[1]

---

[1] When we are not looking, the reality is the reality vectors; when we are looking, we think of the coordinates (the objects).

The Nature of Objects

The roles of the objects in a subsystem become a complicated issue since we are so used to treating the objects as real entities. Their nature may be characterized as:

- The objects are only created as a group to cover the whole domain of the system. The individual object has no meaning, except to show its relation to all other objects.

- The objects in a pattern are not complete or independent. The objects should remain *concealed* in, and cannot emerge from, the system. None of the characteristics of the object can be used to describe the system.

- The proper relationship between the objects will be determined by their interactions. The relationship is the pattern that can represent the system.

To maintain reality in dualism, an object must be *anchored* on its opposite to form a stable pattern. Such anchoring produces characteristics not associated with the objects. In general, an object must be associated with all other objects to represent a system.

We may use music as an example. We may consider individual music notes as objects. A symphony is built on the relationship or the patterns of these notes. The individual notes become concealed and secondary in the representation of the symphony.

All Objects are Interconnected

All objects in the system are interconnected. After such interconnection, they form multiple patterns. Each pattern is independent and shows a specific mode of interconnections.[1] We may see the function of the whole system in any of the patterns. We can also shift to any pattern from any other pattern since all patterns are equivalent.

This concept of multiple inter-connected subsystems is well established in Chinese medicine. In a body, all organs (as subsystems) are interconnected, so an ailment of the stomach may be treated by massaging the bottom of the feet. Each part of the living system is treated as a whole since it is connected through the whole.

In systems thinking, all parts are interconnected. A "complete part" includes its connections to all other parts; so this complete part has become a pattern in our model. Therefore, such a part contains information on all other parts of the system.

---

[1] In mathematical representation, each pattern is a vector in this multi-dimensional space. All vectors are orthogonal to each other.

Systems are not Self-Contradiction

If we think in terms of objects, the system may appear to have "self-contradiction." If we think of the whole system, there is no self-contradiction. The two objects are only used to show the patterns of the whole.

The objects are less than real. Only the objects *plus* their interactions constitute a reality at the object level. The opposite nature of the two objects is harmonized by their interferences. The system as a whole has no intrinsic self-contradiction. Any self-contradiction is an illusion resulting from our habitual dualistic thinking.

As we shall see in our linguistic model, when we render the description of a system in our dualistic language, the description will appear to be fuzzy, self-contradictory, and indeterminate. But, this is because of the dualistic nature of our language. We have to reconstruct the reality from such problematic language expression.

Systems thinking can avoid such dualistic fallacies by considering the objects as constituents to show the patterns. Only the patterns are real.

Unusual Logical Principles

There are many interesting logical consequences from the model or the Aristotle square of oppositions. Many are hidden in the terse texts of Laozi. We show a few examples.

Patterns of Reality

In systems thinking, it is much more convenient to represent an actuality directly in terms of the patterns of the objects. This may release us from the uncertainty in the relationship of the objects in Hard systems thinking.

For example, we may represent an actuality as the following patterns:

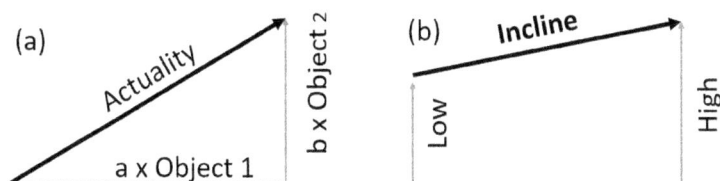

Figure 16   Patterns of Reality

In this pattern representation (a), we are free from the actual meanings of the objects. As stated as one of many examples in Chapter 2 of the *Tao Te Ching*: "high and low" are only used to indicate an *Incline* (b). The two objects must appear at the same time to represent the pattern. For the same reason, we should not think of any *cyclic* transformations between the two objects, or one object is born from the other. The reality must be represented by the complementarity pattern of the two objects.

Laozi uses many examples of different opposite pairs in the *Tao Te Ching* to illustrate this principle of Tao. He characterizes an object as "overflowing" whenever we let the objects stand out. All objects must be concealed.

Opposite Actions are Equivalent

In dualism, we have two actualities to represent the same reality. It may be surprising that not only that the two actualities are equivalent, the two opposite objects also lead to the same logical equivalent if we adhere to the principle of Tao. This deserves our careful consideration.

We may show the system in Figure 17. The two objects are two actions, action A and action B, to realize reality. These two actions will build two equivalent patterns, Pattern A and Pattern B, for reality.

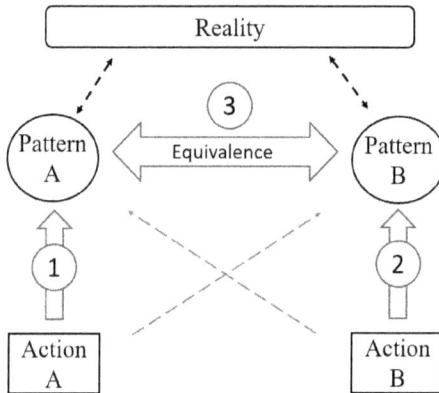

Figure 17   Equivalence of Actions

There are two actualization paths, shown as 1 and 2. Each action will contribute to forming a pattern. There must be also some contribution from the opposite actions (shown as dashed lines) according to the complementary principle.

Therefore, acting with A *following the principle of Tao* will result in pattern A. Since Pattern A and Pattern B are equivalent, doing A and doing B *(following the principle of Tao)* will have equivalent results. The critical condition is that the Actions are executed *according to the principle of Tao* that maintains complementarity. With the guidance of Tao, action A and action B will result in equivalent representations of reality. We may call this the *Principle of Equivalent Actions*.

However, our dualistic mind may fall into a dualistic fallacy and consider these actions (A and B) as different. But, in reality, they are equivalent in the world of Tao. As we have stated in the *Logic of Tao Philosophy*, "acting with Yu 有為" (Yu-wei) and "acting with Wu 無為" (Wu-wei) are both the proper and equivalent ways to execute the principle of Tao.

In Tao philosophy, where and how you start is not important; what is important is that the process of realization must follow the principle of Tao. The result will be the same. This is an answer to the paradoxical question asked by Laozi in Chapter 20: "Yes and no, how much do they differ? Beauty and ugliness, how do they differ?"

An Action leads to the results of its Opposite Action

In a dualistic mind, doing action A will result in the opposite result as doing action B since A and B are opposites. However, in the system of Tao, the result of action A will show the result of action B. This is according to the principle of Tao. This may appear paradoxical.

As shown in Figure 16, action A with proper contribution from action B will result in Pattern A. Pattern A is equivalent to Pattern B and Pattern B will reflect action B with some contribution from action A.

This theme is repeated in many chapters of the *Tao Te Ching*. The pattern is "without doing A, you will get the real result of A." For example, "Without asserting himself, he attracts attention (Chapter 23)." or "Teaching without words (Chapter 2)."

Under such conditions, one action results in its opposite action. We may call this result the *Principle of Reciprocal Actions*. We have to emphasize that this is true only when everything is done according to the principle of Tao.

In a dualistic mind, doing A precludes doing B to happen.

A Pattern must have all Objects

There is another common pattern in the *Tao Te Ching* worthy of some clarification. A pattern must be constructed from all objects. That is, Pattern A cannot be created by action A alone by excluding action B, as shown in Figure 18. There must be contributions from both action A and action B to form Pattern A.

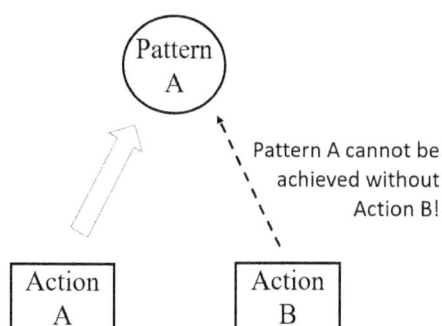

Figure 18   Pattern and Objects

We may see some examples in the *Tao Te Ching*. In Chapter 24, Laozi states: if one tries to show oneself *by excluding the action of "not showing oneself"*, then one cannot be shown clearly. The pattern may also be "by doing A alone, you cannot get A." For example, "By asserting himself, he will not attract attention (Chapter 24)." A pattern cannot be built from action alone.

However, in Chapter 23, Laozi states that, if one is not *just* trying to show oneself *but also includes the action of "not showing oneself"*, then one is shown clearly. Chapter 23 is inclusive of all actions, so the pattern is achieved according to the principle of Tao; Chapter 24 is exclusive of other complementary actions, so the pattern is not achieved.

In many cases in the text of the *Tao Te Ching*, the actuality level and the object level are not distinguished, so the same name, such as heaven and earth, is used as an object or an actuality. This often creates confusion. As in this example, heaven or earth cannot last as an object, but they can last as an actuality.

Only the patterns are real; the objects are not real. This cannot be easily understood because we always think in terms of opposite objects. For example, in Chapter 36 of the *Tao Te Ching*, it has been extremely difficult to understand why an expanding process could exist in a shrinking process. Shrinking and expanding are two objects. The natural phenomena consist of patterns of shrinking and expanding as an actuality.

However, if we think of patterns as reality, then the realistic patterns must consist of shrinking and expanding at the same time. From a systems view, this is quite natural. The fundamental problem is that our dualistic mind thinks of the objects and forgets the reality under discussion.

Non-Local Effects

Complementarity consists of two objects; each object belongs to a sub-domain. There are two segmented parts. Local action on a part will have non-local effects on other parts. A local change will induce a global change.

Holographic Principle

When a three-dimensional object is photographed onto a two-dimensional sheet as a holographic picture. When the sheet is torn into two parts, each part can show the whole object again. It is the holographic principle in which each part can represent the whole.

There is some similarity in Tao philosophy that Tao can manifest equally in Heng Wu and Heng Yu.

Chapter 5
Trichotomy of Time

We expect that part-whole relation to behave with respect to time as it does with respect to space.

Theodore Sider
Four-Dimensionalism, p.87

The logic of dichotomy discussed in the previous chapters may be extended to our understanding of the trichotomy of time. For example, our proper conceptual understanding of the trichotomy of time in terms of "past, present, and future" will directly affect our thinking about the meaning of life.[1]

---

[1] The following discussion was presented at a conference by the author on *Searching for the Meaning of Life* (See publication #4 of the Series).

The topic of time has been an important philosophical issue. We shall review the issue in the logic model. A system with three objects is complicated, but we may simplify the discussions by assuming that the present Now is the doorway between the past and the future. [1] That is, the past and the future can influence each other only through the present. The present is Now.

What is NOW?

How to live in Now has become an important topic in our discussion on the meaning of life. A meaningful life often makes us feel that time is eternal. We often use "Living in Now" to mean that our life is meaningful at the moment.

We face a world with eternal changes, and often fall into anxiety and could not enjoy eternity. We have to eliminate anxiety and let "Living in Now" manifest its meaning, and we can live in Now and feel "eternity and peace." A meaningful Now must be whole.

To completely "Live in Now" transcends the limits of Time and Space. In space, "Living in Now" transcends the dichotomy of "I and the World." In Time, "Living in Now" transcends the Trichotomy of "past, present, and future." To be able to "Live in Now" means that our life at present is complete, meaningful, and eternal.

---

[1] In 2015, the author was surprised to find that the "doorway- state" was also a key assumption in the author's Ph.D. thesis of 1971, which deals with the interactions of three interconnected states of nuclear structure and reaction.

Time as "Past, Present, Future"

In the Hard systems view, Past, Present, and Future are three distinct objects. These objects are interconnected in some unknown way. From our logic model, these objects will form "complementarity" patterns due to their interconnectedness. These patterns are the actualities of time.

We shall identify the Hard systems view of "past, present, and future" as the *Physical Time* at the object level and the realistic representations of time as the *Psychological Time* at the actuality level. The psychological periods become patterns of "the past, the present, and the future."

In the following discussions, we illustrate the concept of Now (the present) in our logic model and the systems view.

Structure of Psychological Time

We habitually segregate time into past, present, and future as three objects. Such a trichotomy breaks time into fragments and thus induces illusions about time in the same way as in dualistic fallacies. Fragments of "past, present, and future" are only concepts at the object level. In Figure 19, we identify these objects as the physical time.

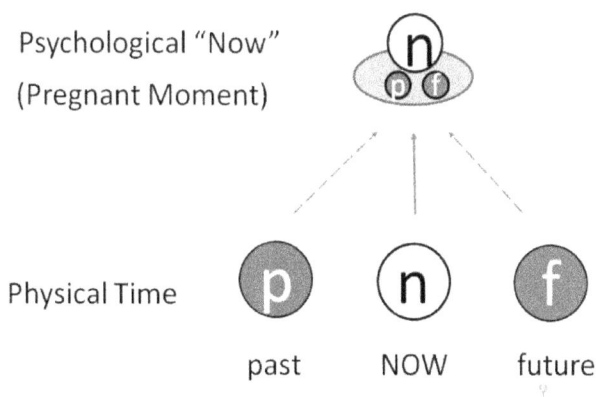

Figure 19 Psychological Time

The fragmentary physical time must be actualized to become a realistic perception of time. Realistic time is our direct apprehension of time, which is the psychological time.[1] In the above figure, we show the psychological time of Now as a superposition of "past, present, future." The structure of psychological time preserves the wholeness of time.

Past, Present, and Future have mutual influences. To make "Now" meaningful for our lives, we have to evaluate our past and future positively in Now. Now may be changed by our new apprehension of our past and our hope for the future. Therefore, a truthful Now must reaffirm our past and hope for our future in the present.

---

[1] In philosophy, there are also A-Theory (similar to Physical Time) and B-Theory (Similar to Psychological Time). Kierkegaard called such a psychological *now* a "Pregnant Moment." In B-Theory, past, present, and future are equally real. M. Taggart called B-theory of time as "block time."

As in systems view, psychological time periods are patterns of the objects: past, present, and future. These patterns reflect the true nature of time. The actualities - the actual past, actual present, and actual future – are just three equivalent representations of reality (time).

Holistic Changes in Time

A realistic Now must be whole and therefore consist of both "changing" and "unchanging" at the same time. Therefore, "Now" is eternal, but is also ceaselessly changing. According to our model, the real Now is "present entangled with past and future" and forms a time packet. A time packet is a pattern of "past, present, future." Such a time packet Now can continue to exist ceaselessly, but its content is ceaselessly changing.

The contents of the time packet may change. That is the objects inside the packet may change, but the pattern is unchanging. This time packet flows as a whole, as shown in the following Figure.

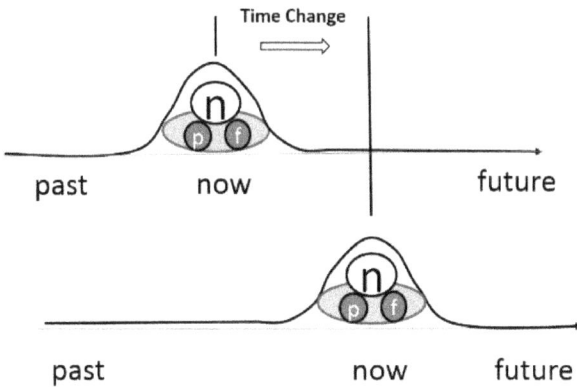

Figure 20 Time Change

This time packet Now behaves like a *moving spotlight* to cover the whole life history in every moment of our life.

Such a time packet Now can continue to exist ceaselessly, but its content is ceaselessly changing. [1] Only in such a "Now," we can maintain its identity with "changing-and-unchanging."

At any moment of Now, we may have a new interpretation of our past and a new vision for our future. The new past and new future are always in harmony with the present to support Now.

---

[1] Both East and West philosophy often describe a reality as "Becoming" and Being." Such separation can easily fall into dualistic fallacies which regard Becoming as always changing and Being as always unchanging. A reality should transcend such dualistic view; a reality must cover Becoming and Being.

From such a time packet, limitless new things (new past, new present, and new future) can appear in Now. Such creativity preserves the Oneness of time and allows us to have flexibility in maintaining a holistic Now.

Such a concept of time is consistent with the principle of Tao. Laozi categorizes such state of eternity as Heng 恆. In the systems view, the objects are changing all the time and we create the patterns of time within us. [1]

---

[1] According to Martin Heidegger we do not exist inside time, *we are time*. Hence, the relationship to the past is a present awareness of *having been*, which allows the past to exist in the present. The relationship to the future is the state of anticipating a potential possibility, task, or engagement. It is related to the human propensity for caring and being concerned, which causes "being ahead of oneself" when thinking of a pending occurrence. Therefore, this concern for a potential occurrence also allows the future to exist in the present. (Wikipedia, TIME)

Chapter 6
Ancient Systems Philosophers

Here we shall discuss a few philosophers whose thinking patterns may be considered as systems thinking. They deal with the roles of the parts in the whole. They have similar views on the interactions between the parts.

In Western philosophy, most treat objects with dualistic nature and their interactions. For Heraclitus, the material world consists of opposite conditions and tendencies which, nevertheless, are held in unity by hidden harmony. The hidden harmony of opposites of Heraclitus is called the "logos." Empedocles (492-430 BCE) introduced "love" for attraction and "hatred" for repulsion. Parmenides seems to consider the interactions as a harmonizing force, i.e., without dualistic nature.

In Eastern philosophy, the interactions between the objects are harmonization to support nature. It is mainly a systems view of nature as one.

We may show that both Western and Eastern philosophies are based on the concept of Oneness. Prime examples are Parmenides, the Buddha, and Laozi. Their philosophical roots are similar. They appear in the same period of history.

In the following discussions, we shall only highlight their common basic features and ignore their differences in many interpretations.

Parmenides

Parmenides (515 - 450 BCE) was a Greek philosopher and poet at Elea in lower Italy. His poem *On Nature* describes his systems view. His main concept is the *Oneness* of nature. Unfortunately, his view has not been consistently comprehended and his logic is generally thought of as extremely abstract.

His poem of about 160 verses starts with a Prologue that proclaims that there are *two ways of inquiry* into everything and we can seek the truth in *both* of them. His Goddess emphasizes that *these two ways must be pursued at the same time*. Parmenides has the *way of truth* and the *way of opinion:*

- In the *way of truth* (the one that is based on what-is), we look for "the unshaken heart of well-rounded reality (*Aletheia*)" or "true reality." This is based on Oneness where "motion and change" are impossible. In the *way of truth*, we are looking at the WHAT-IS as a whole, "which is collected together".

- In the *way of opinion* (the one that is not), we are "two-headed" and think based on dualistic thinking of the mortals' opinions (Doxa), "which is scattered everywhere".

Parmenides distinguishes his authentic thinking (*nous*) from the thinking that splits and differentiates.

In the *way of truth*, we view the system directly in terms of actualities which are *what-is*. In the *way of opinion*, we deal with objects which are *what-is-not*. The actualities are beings; the objects are non-beings, in Parmenides' words.

With our model, we may identify the two ways of seeking truth as the way of actualities (idealism) and the way of the objects (materialism). Parmenides is a unified theorist of ancient idealism and materialism (realism).[1]

The Way of Truth

Parmenides associates our thought with immediate apprehension of reality and, therefore, thought should exist only for what is real. The goddess then urges us to observe how things absent (of objects) can be securely present to the mind. We may begin our search for truth from anywhere and we shall return to the same point. In our model, all actualities are equivalent and all actions will lead to the same truth if done properly.

---

[1] Parmenides is often taken to be the father of idealism, especially after Plato came to regard his Being as the forms. His second way of seeking truth has grossly been neglected. In the very beginning of his poem, he actually stated that both ways must be pursued. Our model shows that his two ways are valid (as the systems and the scientific views of nature).

We shall refer to WHAT-IS as *being* and WHAT-IS-NOT as *not-being*. The fundamental concept of Parmenides is WHAT-IS. When we think of reality, we can only think of its manifestations as actualities, which are beings. Being appears to be absent (of objects) only because it is well-rounded, but it can be well secured in our thought. To think in terms of What-Is is the *way of truth*.

The Way of Opinion

After the goddess discussed the signposts of Being, she started to discuss the *way of opinion* (*Doxa*) as the second way of inquiry into the Truth. [1]

The *way of opinion* has been a point of disagreement in much scholastic discourse. This way is often treated as based on "false opinions." We see it in a *positive* way based on the objects and their interactions. With such a mindset, we may interpret the whole poem in a consistent framework.

For example, the mortals often wander with two heads – i.e., holding two opposite views in their mind. They become perplexed by their senses which will steer their intelligence astray. Such acts carry them along, deaf and blind, dazed, with the uncritical crowds. The mortals consider everything as opposite objects, which are *what-is-not*. Parmenides reminds us again that the view that WHAT-IS-NOT, should not predominate.

---

[1] This way must also be pursued. It is unfortunate that many believed the second part of Parmenides' poem is incomplete and fragmentary.

In the *way of opinion*, we should avoid being driven by our ordinary experiences along that way based on the objects that have no reality. We should not let these ordinary experiences, the eye that is actually sightless, the ear that is already full, and the tongue, to rule. The way to think in terms of What-Is-Not is the Way of opinion.

The Key Fragment

As an introduction to the *way of opinion*, the goddess proclaims that mortal men have customarily named things in two forms (as two opposite forms). This is where they have gone astray.[1] In systems thinking, Parmenides' statement is equivalent to:

> If we characterize a system with two objects and consider these two objects as real, our minds will go astray.

This is equivalent to stating that we should not take the pair of objects to be real. With such a warning, the second part of Parmenides' poem may be interpreted consistently. Parmenides then talks about the complementarity nature of the objects. His philosophy can be readily brought into a sharp focus as a whole.

---

[1] This fragment is a key fragment that shows the basic reason that we can go astray with the way of opinion. This fragment has been interpreted in some other forms and may have led to incoherent interpretation of the second part of the Parmenides' poem. Based on the above interpretation, the second part provides a coherent description of the way of truth based on mortals' opinions.

The Logic of Parmenides

We may seek truth by the *way of truth* at the actuality level or we may seek truth by the *way of opinion* at the object level. In our model, the actuality level and the object level equally represent the two ways to seek reality. We may summarize the logic structure of Parmenides in Figure 21.

Truth		
The Phenomenal World	**The Way of Truth**	**What-Is** (Systems, Actualities)
	The Way of Opinion	**What-Is-Not** (Objects)

Figure 21 Parmenides' Two Ways of Truth

The way of truth is based on What-is. What-is are the actualities that can represent reality. The way of opinion is based on what-is-not. What-is-not is objects, which are not reality. The reality is superimposed of two opposite objects, like day and night. The day is embedded in the night, as " the moon shines with borrowed light." The two opposite objects are complementary to describe the actualities.

We may show the Parmenides model in Figure 22.

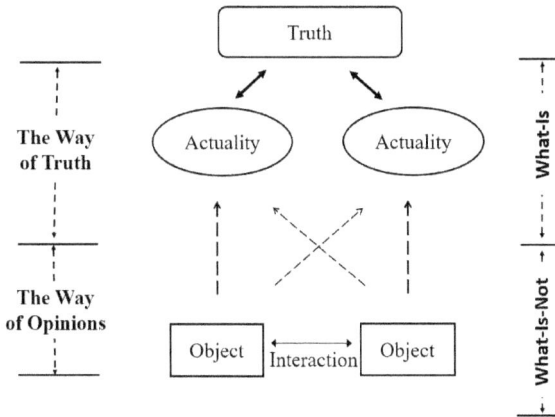

Figure 22 What-Is and What-Is-Not

Parmenides describes how the mortals first contrast phenomena with opposite, distinctive, and independent signs. These signs are the actualities. This is the description of the actuality level. Each sign is uniform and distinct everywhere - the same as itself in every direction and not the same as the other; so each sign is treated as complete and independent by itself.

At the actuality level, the key concept is the Oneness of all beings. When we describe a being with two opposites, then the being is full equality of the two opposites; neither one of the opposites should not overshadow the other. Parmenides called this the "well-rounded nature of each being," each being is full of the two opposites. Each being should have both opposites equally. This is how Parmenides describes the actualities.

At the object level, the objects are not real, so Parmenides calls them what-is-not. Parmenides uses an example of bright sky and dark night to show how these two opposites (the objects) should be related. The goddess describes the interactions as the divine order and she uses "Love" to symbolize a binding force between two opposites as male and female.

Parmenides also describes the process of actualization as the mating of males and females. When these two elements are mixed as seeds of Love, they will mold well-constituted bodies (the truth) if they are in the right proportion. Otherwise, they will harm the growing embryo.

It is interesting to note that he does not use dualistic interaction as "love and hate." His law of interaction is love. He seems to regard the interactions as harmonization of the opposites.

Parmenides' Principle of Oneness

It is also interesting that Parmenides has a detailed description of the principle of Oneness. The basic world order is: "Being is well rounded and has perfect symmetry everywhere." The goddess repeats that we describe things in two extreme opposites, but we cannot have one overshadowing the other. The two opposites are in complementarity:

> And when all things have been named Light and Night, and things corresponding to their powers have been assigned to each, everything is full of light and obscure night at once, both are equal.

This echoes Laozi's words that the myriad things are born in Wu and born in Yu equally. All parts contribute to the whole.

The goddess shows how the cosmic order is reflected in men's conduct. Our mind works in the same way as our limbs and our head do. We think in two inter-related ways. We may think in various individual ways as how limbs work and we may also think as a whole as how our head works. Limbs work individually but are related to the head.

Parmenides emphasizes that the object level and the actual level are equivalent. He says that "It is the same thing to think as a whole or individually; only the combined result emerges as a complete Thought." Both levels can represent Oneness.

Summary on Parmenides

We are surprised to see that the poem of Parmenides may be interpreted very consistently with our model.

Parmenides emphasizes the need to maintain the "unity of opposites" view within his holistic thinking of *Being*. He recognizes the world appearances or opinions of mortals, as an important way to gain the truth, if wholeness of Being is retained.

Parmenides is a key figure in the development of Pre-Socratic thought, with abstract thinking. Parmenides' writing has survived in a reasonably full and coherent form. The poem is vividly written and the reader should read it in its complete form.

Our interpretation may serve as a possibility to resolve many perplexing speculations on Parmenides' logic, see Zeno paradoxes in Appendix B. In our view, he does not discount the world appearances and considers it an important way to gain the truth. Truth is expressed equally in the opposites that have to be viewed with Oneness.

The Buddha

In this section, we shall present a summary of the basic logic of Buddhist philosophy. Buddhist thoughts have a long history and many ways of interpretation. We shall only present the view related to our logic model. Many of the discussions are greatly simplified.

In Buddhism, we may identify two levels of truth in the phenomenal world as the *Nirvana* and *Samsara* levels. In Samsara, people hang on to illusionary objects and their interactions. In Nirvana, people can fully realize the *dependent origination* of the objects and attain a state that is free from individual objects. The objects are empty of self-nature, and the actualities are empty of objects. The states of nirvana are the actualities 實相 in our model.

In Buddhism, the objects are said to lack *self-nature* (*svabhava*). All objects are dependently *co-arising* (*pratitya-samutpada*) and, if properly correlated, they can form non-substantial states of truth – the actualities. These states represent what we can consciously experience from the *ultimate truth*. The truth at the object level is the *conventional truth*. The ultimate truth is free from any object. Therefore, we may identify nirvana as the actuality level and samsara as the object level. The absolute reality is Emptiness. The basic structure may be shown in Figure 23.

Levels	Contents	Characteristics
Reality	Emptiness	Buddha-nature, Oneness, Self-nature
Ultimate Truth (Nirvana)	Actualities	Wisdom, true nature, empty of objects, Rta, Patterns of dependent origination, wholeness, Non-substantial. 空
Conventional Truth (Samsara)	Objects	Co-arising, no self-nature, no intrinsic properties, impermanence (duhkha), False names, Substance, Senses. Maya, 色

Figure 23 Basic Buddhism Structure

The principle of Buddhism is Oneness, which is called *Emptiness* (*sunyata*). The principle of Buddhist logic is the reality of the Buddha's nature. The absolute reality is often characterized as *Emptiness*. For convenience, we identify this core principle as the Oneness of nature. Reality is One, which is formless and empty of any form.

In this structure, we have identified the state of Nirvana as the Ultimate Truth, and the state of Samsara as the Conventional Truth. This is the *Doctrine of Two Truths*. The Samsara view is the object level and the Nirvana view is the actuality level. The actualities are the views of the system.[1]

Two Levels of Truth

Nirvana and Samsara equivalently describe the same reality in different ways. Nagarjuna says, "The limit of nirvana is the limit of samsara. Between the two there is not the slightest bit of difference." These limits refer to the principle of Oneness.

Samsara can be transformed into nirvana through an enlightenment process as prescribed by the teachings of the Buddha. The objects have forms and the actualities are formless. In Buddhism, forms and formless (emptiness) are two equivalent ways to view reality: Ultimately, emptiness is form and form is emptiness. This is consistent with our logic model.

---

[1] It is also possible to interpret Nirvana and Samsara as two actualities such as the Heng Wu and the Heng Yu; this would also result in two truths. Some interpretation regard Nirvana as Wu and Samsara as Yu, but such interpretation can easily fall into dualistic fallacies and should be avoided.

- Nirvana means awakening to the true nature of the phenomenal world. This is the perfection of Buddha's wisdom in the world. This perfection is regarded as requiring the elimination of earthly desires for objects. In Nirvana, the actualities are empty of objects. As in systems view, the objects are only chosen form patterns that can represent reality. Buddhism even considers the patterns as ultimately false because they are based on objects.
- Samsara is the state characterized as impermanence (*duhkha*) in the phenomenal world. Nothing lasts. Our inability to understand this impermanence leads to our suffering. The root cause of samsara is the discriminating mind that holds on to the impermanent objects. In Samsara, the objects have no self-nature, are co-arising, dependent origination, and impermanence, etc. The objects change ceaselessly and Samsara results in rounds of rebirth.

The objects are only conveniently chosen as a group to represent the whole. The objects are false names (without authenticity). The reality is empty of any properties associated with the objects.

Enlightenment Process

According to the Buddhist teachings, we can release these objects from our minds and treat them as empty of self-nature. We can enlighten our minds to see reality by shifting our minds from the objects to the actualities. Enlightenment is a process of integration to reach Nirvana from Samsara.

Both Samsara and Nirvana levels cover the whole domain and they are equivalent ways to represent the same reality. The process may be shown in the following figure:

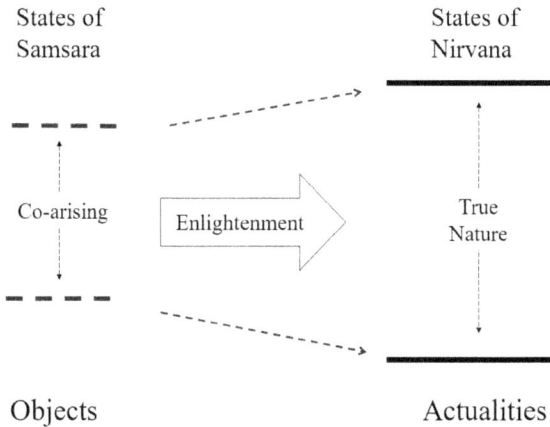

Figure 24   Enlightening Process

The process is an actualization process, bound by the principle of Oneness, or the Dharmas in Buddhism. In this model, the states of Samsara are equivalent to the state of interacting objects. The objects are impermanent due to their interactions. The states of Nirvana are fully interconnected patterns of objects. These two levels describe the same reality in different ways.

The Doctrine of Two Truths

Nagarjuna identifies two truths as the *Conventional Truth* and the *Ultimate Truth*. He also recognizes that the Ultimate Truth cannot be obtained independently of the Conventional Truth, and Nirvana is not obtained without Samsara.

In reality, these two truths are equivalent: Based on the Conventional, the Ultimate is taught; based on the Ultimate, the Conventional is taught. Nagarjuna says:

> If we do not understand the conventional truth, then we cannot understand the ultimate truth; if we cannot understand the ultimate truth, we cannot attain Nirvana.

Therefore, in the phenomenal world, both Samsara and Nirvana are two equivalent ways of truth. The two levels (*Samsara* and *Nirvana*) are not dealing with two separate realities; both ways observe the same common condition: Oneness.[1] Nagarjuna says, "As for all dependent origination, I would call them emptiness." Form and emptiness seem two opposites, but, in systems view, "Form is Emptiness and Emptiness is Form."[2]

The ultimate goal is to achieve the ultimate truth where we do not hold any individual image as reality. Nagarjuna explains the ultimate truth with the negation of all dualistic object designations. Such negation becomes the self-nature of emptiness.

All designations of names in the phenomenal world are "false names," but they are nevertheless useful and necessary. This is the foundation of the teachings of the Buddha.

---

[1] There are many such dual equivalent ways of seeking the truth whenever two opposite ways are chosen. We may realize enlightenment via a "Being-way" (The Way of Wu) of Zen meditation (禪定) or a "Folk-way" (the Way of Yu) of precepts (持戒). Both ways are valid and practiced.

[2] Nagarjuna treats senses as form 色 and the reality as emptiness 空. These two are at the same level of reality and there is no ontological priority.

The Middle Way

The Doctrine of Two Truths is the core of the Middle Way. The Middle Way is to include both the Ultimate Truth and the Conventional Truth. It is to avoid choosing one over the other, as done in many ancient Indian philosophical traditions.

The Dharma: The Laws of Interactions

The teaching of Buddha is called the *Dharmas*, which may be considered as the principle of Buddhism. Dharmas also refer to the laws of interaction between objects.[1] The roles of Dharmas are similar to the Te in Tao philosophy.

The Buddhist teachings (The Dharmas) pave a way for us to be free of the bondage of objects and to reach the states of nirvana. The Dharmas is the laws of all interactions at the object level and the condition of Oneness at all level.

Summary on Buddhism

In Buddhism, we may apply the same Principle of Oneness to all views. With our model, we may summarize the logic of Buddhist philosophy with the following characteristics:

---

[1] The concept of Dharmas appear in many ways. For our purpose, it is the overall principle and teachings of Buddhism. It is the laws of interactions at the object level. It is the self-nature of reality.

- Two Ways of Seeking Truth – We may seek the Ultimate Truth in the Conventional Truth or vice versa.
- The Opposite Objects are Complementary – All objects in the states of samsara are co-arising and complementary. Their complementarities form the states of nirvana.
- The Actualities are Equivalent – There are many states of nirvana. All nirvana states represent the same reality with different but equivalent characteristics.
- A Teleological Force and The Principle of Oneness – The teachings of the Buddha are based on detaching from illusionary objects. The teleological forces are prescribed in the Dharmas. There is an overall principle that governs reality. In Buddhism, this principle is the Doctrine of Emptiness. The teleological forces drive our thinking toward emptiness.

These are the guideline on how our model can be applied to the Buddhist philosophy of the Middle Way. The Middle Way is inclusive of the two ways, not exclusive of the two ways.

Laozi

We have used the logic of Tao philosophy as the base in our model discussed in Chapter 3, so the logic model is fully embedded in Tao philosophy. We shall use this section as a summary of Laozi's logic system. For a full discussion, refer to the *Logic of Tao Philosophy*.

In the first chapter of the *Tao Te Ching*, we first assume that we may describe the nature of the myriad things as Wu (totally without differentiation) or Yu (totally with differentiation).[1] In this dualistic view, they are either the same or different.

However, the reality is that the myriad things are neither totally the same nor different. In other words, the true states are: the myriad things are the same in some aspects *and* different in some other aspect, at the same time. Laozi has designated these true states as the *Heng Wu* and the *Heng Yu*. Laozi describes these states in Chapter one of the *Tao Te Ching*.

---

[1] It is interesting to point out that "Wu and Yu" has the same meaning as "One and the many" relationship. Wu is One without differentiation and Yu is the Many with differentiation. "One and the Many" relationship may be expressed in our logic odel.

Chapter One of the *Tao Te Ching*

Laozi very skillfully uses the following paragraphs to describe the true relationship between the myriad things: the *Heng Wu* and the *Heng Yu*. After defining Wu and Yu, Laozi describes *Heng Wu* and *Heng Yu* as:

- In *Heng Wu*, we first see no differences among the myriad things, but the myriad things appear to show some differences. That is, in *Heng Wu*, we see the subtle appearance of Yu. Therefore, the *Heng Wu* is the state of Wu anchored on Yu.

- In *Heng Yu*, we first see the distinct differences of the myriad things, but the boundaries of the myriad things appear to fade away. That is, in *Heng Yu*, we see the subtle appearance of Wu. Therefore, the *Heng Yu* is the state of Yu anchored on Wu.

Therefore, the reality is a pattern of objects in complementarity: One object must be anchored on its opposite to be real. The objects Wu and Yu cannot represent reality, but their complementarity can represent reality. The complementarities are the actualities *Heng Wu* and *Heng Yu*.

Both the objects and the actualities are dualistic but have a very different nature. In Tao philosophy, Wu and Yu are the two objects in *traditional dualism* and the actualities *Heng Wu* and *Heng Yu* are the actualities in *ontological dualism*. In ontological dualism, the two actualities are equivalent (See Page 70).

Laozi repeatedly warns against taking any object to be real, but he recognizes the usefulness of the objects in the actualities. Laozi uses many examples of different pairs of objects to show the principle of Tao.

Square of Opposition

Interestingly, the two kinds of dualism in Tao philosophy may be expressed in the traditional square of the opposition of Aristotle. The relationship between the actualities and the objects can be expressed as the four corners of the square of oppositions. The four corners are:

- Yu is universal affirmative where everything is differentiated;
- Wu is universal negative where nothing is differentiated;
- Heng Yu is particular affirmative where something is differentiated, but some are not;
- Heng Wu is particularly negative where something is not differentiated, but some are.

In the square, Wu and Yu are *contrary* and *Heng Wu* and *Heng Yu* are *subcontrary*. That is, the objects are *contrary opposites*, but the actualities are *subcontrary opposites*. It also shows that the two subcontrary opposites may be both true, as stated by Laozi that the two actualities *Heng Wu* and *Heng Yu* are equivalent representations of Tao.

For a more detailed description of the Square of Opposition, see Appendix A.

The Structure of Tao Logic

Tao philosophy is a way to preserve reality in dualistic thinking. Laozi starts with traditional dualistic thinking and shows how we can preserve reality in a logic that can express the actualities in terms of the objects.

Interaction and Linguistic Models

As shown in Chapter 3, we may use an *Interaction Model* to find the relationship between actualities and objects. The actualities are the manifestations of Tao as *Heng Wu* and *Heng Yu*. The objects are Wu and Yu. The interactions are introduced between Wu and Yu to ensure that the object level is not fragmented. The Interaction Model with Laozi terminology is shown in Figure 25.

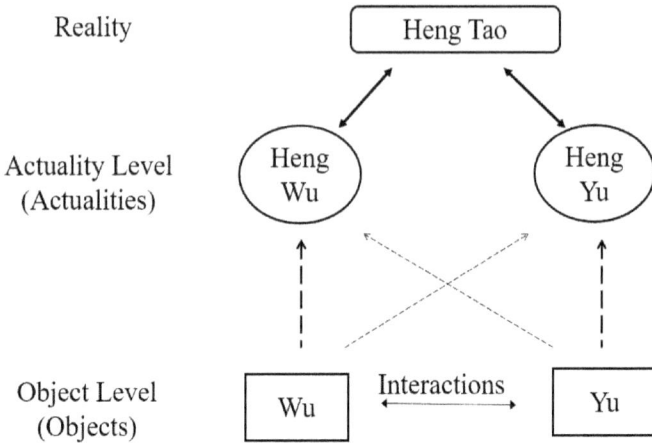

Figure 25   Interaction Model

The result of the interactions is that the objects are *superimposed* to form the patterns of actualities. The mathematical result is:

$$< \text{Heng Wu} > \quad = \quad a < \text{Wu} > \; + \; b < \text{Yu} >$$

$$< \text{Heng Yu} > \quad = \quad a < \text{Yu} > \; - \; b < \text{Wu} >$$

Equation 4 Structure of Actualities

Equation 4 is the same as Equation 1 on page 64. These equations show that the patterns of actualities in terms of objects. The basic structure is the complementarity of the objects. We have discussed the logical consequences in the previous chapters. The actualities will have properties that none of the objects has.

In Laozi's words, the objects are rigid and strong but these characteristics will disappear or become soft and tender within the actualities. The reality is not reflected by the properties of the objects but is reflected in the structure or patterns of the objects.

As shown on page 81, the Linguistic Model will take Wu and Yu as simple concepts that have been commonly accepted and are directly expressed in our language. The actualities are complex concepts that can be conceptually expressed in terms of the superposition of objects.

The linguistic expression of the actualities will be vague, self-contradictory, and indeterminate, as shown in the words of Laozi. However, his words show accurately the structure of logic in Tao philosophy.

Tao as a System

Tao is a system of Oneness. The word Heng 恆 is the central concept of the logic of Tao philosophy. This means that reality must be whole and cannot be divided. For simplicity, we have interpreted this word as True or Holistic.

At the systems level, both *Heng Wu* and *Heng Yu* are fully integrated subsystems that can represent the living system. All entities at this level have wholeness and are real.

At the object level, the two opposite objects refer to the basic possible nature of the myriad things. These objects describe the sub-domains for the parts only and cannot represent the reality of Tao as a whole.

To restore wholeness at the object level, the objects must be interconnected through their interactions. The law of these interactions is called Te 德 in Tao philosophy. Such interactions appear as the power of Tao imposed on the objects to maintain the harmony of all objects.

This law of interactions acts as the teleological driving force to ensure that the objects will form the actualities that are real and free from interactions. It is also due to such interactions, the objects form entangled patterns to represent the system.

Tao philosophy is based on dualism. In dualism, there will be two equivalent representations for a reality. They represent genuine synonymies, as multiple states of the Being. We can shift back and forth between these two patterns, without any effort. The two patterns are expressed in terms of the networked relationship of the objects.

Summary on Tao Philosophy

We may say that the systems view of Laozi is in the concept of Heng 恆 of Tao philosophy. Heng is wholeness and cannot be easily described or translated, but it has a well-defined meaning in the logic structure in Tao philosophy.

After our analysis, we are convinced that Laozi has followed the proper logic to describe the manifestations of Tao. Therefore, we should not randomly speculate on the vague and indeterminate words of Laozi. With systems thinking, we can avoid the traditional problems of dualistic fallacies. Systems thinking seems to be an alternative way to see how his words bear the truth of Tao with precision.

In the systems view, the characteristics of the myriad things are not fuzzy and indeterminate. Both the traditional views and the views of the system complement each other. We can then appreciate the ultimate order of Oneness as prescribed by Laozi.

Chapter 7 Summary

It is complementarity all the way.

The logic model discussed in this book is general and maybe a solution to "the one and the many" problem of Aristotle. The model may be applied to many philosophical investigations of multiplicities.

We discuss the relation of the parts and the whole in terms of the general characteristics of systems thinking and the logic principle derived from the Tao philosophy. Systems thinking can be a very good tool in resolving many dualistic paradoxes.

We recognize that a living system and reality share the same function for its survival. Reality is a living system that can manifest in many ways, as many actualities. Each actuality is a self-making organization of concepts to represent reality. Reality will self-actualize within the principle of Oneness since a reality must have oneness.

In systems thinking, we start with the function of a system and then discuss the subsystems to support the function, which is a reality. Science traverses in a reversed direction, from interacting objects to showing the function of the system. We have shown that these two approaches are equivalent and may be discussed within the same logic model.

A reality and a living system that share the same logic patterns will preserve the whole. Whenever we look at a living system, we look at networked patterns of objects; whenever we think of reality, we think of networked patterns of ideas. Systems thinking is an important complementary view to Hard systems thinking.

Dualistic Pitfalls

Systems thinking can help avoid many pitfalls. In traditional dualism, we often treat objects as real and take the opposite objects to mean independent things. However, the objects are not real. Our logic model shows that the objects are only parts, but their patterns may be used to represent reality.

All objects must appear at the same time and, therefore, there is no possibility of cyclic transitions between the objects. The notion of cyclic transitions has been the cause for many puzzles, such as the question of chicken and egg: Which object comes first? Objects cannot be taken as the cause and the effect since they are not real. We have to avoid *traditional dualism* and think in terms of *ontological dualism*.

The pitfalls may be easily avoided in systems thinking, there is no cyclic change of objects in the patterns and objects must be in complementarity and cannot be associated with cause and effect. Sometimes the pitfalls are very hard to recognize, such as the ones in Zeno's paradoxes.

Many Worlds Theory

In systems thinking, we may choose many equivalent sets of objects to represent the same reality. For different sets of objects, there will be different patterns that can represent equally the system. Therefore, there are many worlds of different sets of objects and each set will have many patterns.

The real world will appear as many worlds and all world representations are equally valid.

The basic units of the world are the objects in various patterns. These objects are socially and culturally determined. This is the basis for a pluralistic society. The only condition is that the world is One.

Interactions and Patterns

Objects and patterns may change, so the world appears changing all the time. The principle remains the same. The Hard systems view observes the changes in the objects and the systems view observes the changes in the patterns.

The objects and the patterns are equivalent. The interactions of the objects determine the patterns and the patterns impose the conditions for the interactions. Both the interactions and the patterns are bound by the same principle.

We also can switch our view of reality from the objects to the patterns, and vice versa. They are equivalent.

In systems thinking, the objects are just abstract units for building the patterns of subsystems to support the system.

Traditional Philosophy

The relationship between systems thinking and Hard systems thinking is similar to traditional materialism (realism) and idealism.

Realism is to assert that physical objects are universals that enjoy an "independent" existence. That is like the mechanistic view. Idealism is like the systems view that reality is the patterns of organization of objects. In short, our logic model reflects both the systems view and the mechanistic view in one framework.

The two levels, objects, and actualities, in our model, are also used in the theory of forms of Plato and many other philosophers.

Traditional Sciences

In scientific thinking, we try to determine the nature of the objects and their interactions to instruct a system. The interactions between scientific objects are imposed by theoretical considerations.   In systems thinking, the properties of the subsystems are imposed from the overall system.

Both the living principle and the physical theory are bound by the wholeness of the system. The two approaches are two ways to interpret the same logic model. Both approaches can be complementary. The two approaches are often used simultaneously in our searching path for reality.

Modern sciences have overcome the duality of particle and wave, duality of mass and energy, duality of time and space, etc. Quantum theory and Relativity have shown many non-dualistic phenomena, which may be used to understand the paradoxes in our logic model of Tao philosophy.

Linguistic Description of a Reality

Our model shows why our language is always inadequate in describing reality. However, we should not ignore the "fuzzy, self-contradictory, and indeterminate" descriptions of reality. These are the proper ways to express reality in our language.

We should attempt to build patterns from the fuzzy linguistic description. With the guidance of our logic model, we have consistently interpreted the terse and paradoxical verses of the *Tao Te Ching*.

The Tai-Chi Patterns

We have found that the same principle is repeated at descending scales form a living system through the subsystems and then to the objects. At every step, there are multiple states that a system may take. The same force, a teleological force driving all to One, is active at all steps.

In dualism, the patterns are complementarity as shown in the Tai-chi Diagram. In breaking down a system, the system will generate complementarity pairs. Each part looks just like a small wholeness that can be broken into a similar smaller pair. Mandelbrot illustrates this property as "self-similarity." The two subsystems resulting from the reproductive fracture have similar organization patterns. They have structural aspects also different from the system and from one another.

It is complementarity all the way.

In our model of process philosophy, the structural change in a subsystem is under the constraint of the principle of Oneness. The subsystem may change, but the patterns remain the same since the patterns have to reflect the same system. The structural change that occurs in the subsystem may be triggered by internal re-arrangement of objects or by interactions with its environment.

Aristotle's Square of Opposition

It was quite interesting to realize that Laozi's logic structure in the first chapter of the *Tao Te Ching* is consistent with Aristotle's square of opposition.

The two subcontraries, *Heng Wu* and *Heng Yu*, are both true under the condition that Tao is One and the principle of Oneness is preserved in our thinking.

Systems Thinking and Logic of Tao Philosophy

The concepts in systems thinking can provide an alternative framework for many philosophical discourses and can unify our concepts of the parts and the whole. Systems thinking is a complement to traditional Hard systems thinking. Systems thinking serves as a platform to understand the logic model which is first recognized in the Tao philosophy.

Systems thinking has shed additional light and simplified our previous understanding of the logic of Tao philosophy. We have now a consistent logic model that can avoid some common paradoxes in dualism.

Appendix A:
Square of Opposition

The doctrine of the square of opposition originated with Aristotle in the fourth century BC and has occurred in logic texts ever since. The model has not been widely popularized. We found this model only near the end of our investigation of Tao philosophy. Our model has great similarity to the traditional square of opposition of Aristotle.

Square of Opposition

The traditional square is represented by four forms: (1) the universal positive A, (2) universal negative E, (3) particular positive I, and (4) particular negative O. The square are shown in Figure 26.

The *doctrine* of Aristotle contains three claims: that **A** and **O** are contradictories, that **E** and **I** are contradictories, and that **A** and **E** are contraries.

Figure 26 1

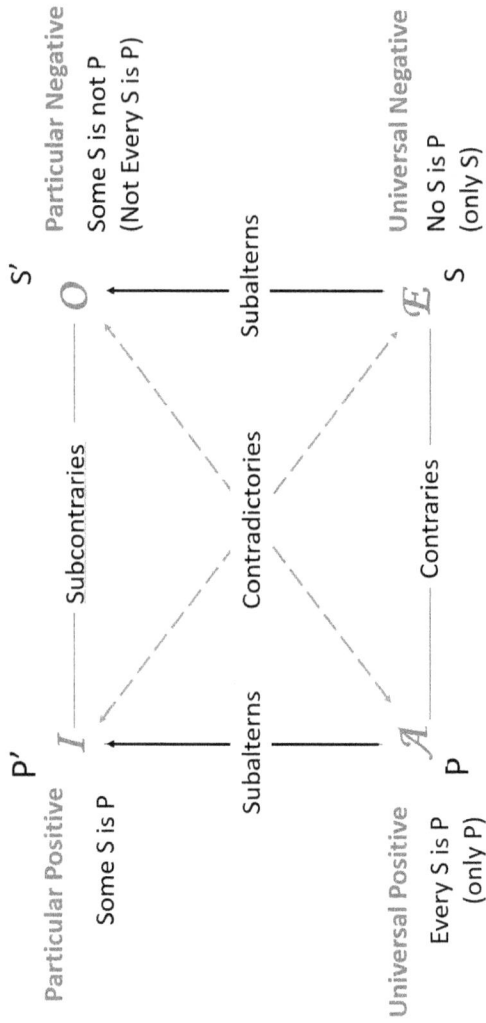

The propositions are placed in the four corners of a square, and the relations are represented as lines drawn between them. In summary:

- Universal statements are contraries: P and S cannot be true together. They are contraries.
- Particular statements are *subcontraries*: P' and S' cannot be false together, but could be both true. In our model, they are both true for the complete complementarity. Since subcontraries are *negations of universal statements*, they were called 'particular' statements.
- The particular statement of one quality is the *subaltern* of the universal statement of that same quality, which is the *superaltern* of the particular statement. Alternation is a relation between a particular statement and a universal statement of the same quality such that the particular is implied by the other.
- The universal affirmative and the particular negative are contradictory.

Aristotle's articulation of the **O** form is *not* the familiar 'Some *S* is not *P*'; it is rather 'Not every *S* is *P*'.

Relation to Our model

We may show the relationship between the actualities, *Heng Wu* and *Heng Yu*, and the objects, Wu and Yu, in terms of the traditional square of oppositions. We may show the Logic of Tao philosophy in Figure 26.

Figure 2?

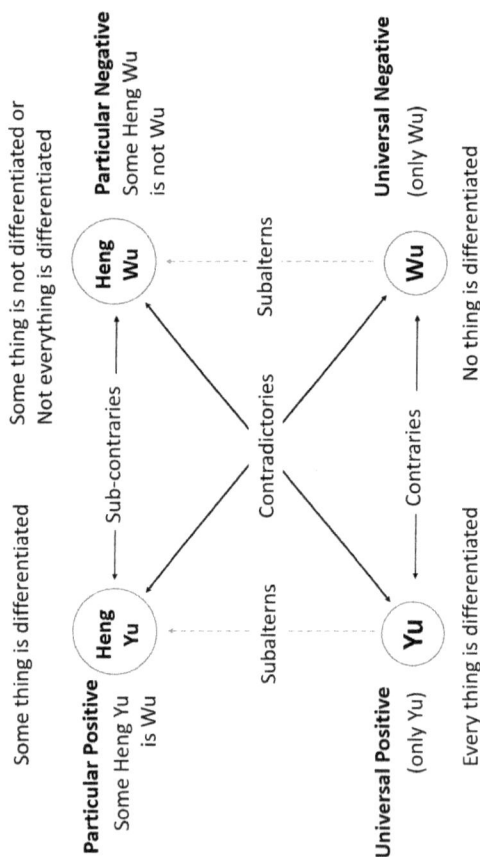

P is differentiation. S is the negation of differentiation. Yu is affirmation and Wu is negation. There are four corners:

- Universal Affirmative (P) - the state of Yu; everything is differentiated
- Universal Negative (S) – the state of Wu; nothing is differentiated;
- Particular Affirmative (O) - the state of *Heng Yu*; something is differentiated, but not all are;
- Particular Negative (I) - the state of *Heng Wu*; something is not differentiated, but some are.

Wu and Yu are contraries; *Heng Wu* and *Heng Yu* are subcontraries. Two propositions are subcontraries if and only if they cannot both be false but can both be true.

It may be paradoxical that two different or "opposite" actualities, *Heng Wu* and *Heng Yu*, are equivalent. *They are equivalent only when they are complementary and both are whole according to the principle of Oneness.*

The two actualities are *subcontrary opposites* and maybe both true. For example, "The cup is half full" and "The cup is half empty" are equivalent. Although "full" and "empty" are opposite, when we refer to the whole cup, the two statements are equivalent. They are equivalent because they have the structure of *complementarity* of the two objects. Not all subcontraries are equivalent.

The equivalence of *Heng Wu* and *Heng Yu* in Tao philosophy is consistent with this ancient square of opposition in Western philosophy.

Appendix B:
Systems Thinking on
Zeno Paradoxes

*Paradoxes appear whenever
Oneness is not observed.*

*Zeno attempts to show that, if we assume
multiplicities are real, contradictions
will appear.*

Zeno's Paradoxes

Zeno (ca. 490–430 BC) introduces three paradoxes as a set of philosophical problems to support Parmenides' logic of Oneness. These paradoxes are Achilles and the Tortoise, the Dichotomy argument, and an Arrow in Flight.

Numerous proposals since Aristotle and Archimedes have not resolved the paradoxes. Most proposals deal with issues of divisibility of space and time. Many fall into the dualistic pitfalls in the very first step of addressing the central point in Zeno's arguments.

However, there have been a few comments that might have led to our conclusions based on systems thinking. For examples:

- Aristotle remarked that as the distance decreases, the time needed to cover those distances also decreases so that the time needed also becomes increasingly small.
- Hans Reichenbach has proposed that the paradox may arise from considering space and time as separate entities.

We shall not review the historical proposals from mathematicians, philosophers, and scientists to resolve these paradoxes. Many of these analyses are quite elaborate.[1] Instead, we want to propose our solutions based on the observation from systems views on these paradoxes.

The Zeno Time System

The Zeno system deals with the fact that someone is moving at some *speed*. The system reality is the *speed* of the entities in the system.

That speed must be the pattern that needs to be preserved in all discussions. The pattern of speed is *"distance"* over *"time."* In our model, distance and time are two objects that can form the pattern of speed. The objects "distance" and "time" are not real; they are the non-beings in Parmenides' language. Only the Being (speed) is real. When we take either the distance or time to be individually real, we shall go astray.

The first two paradoxes appear because we take "distance" to be independently real by ignoring "time," and thus ignoring the system reality of "speed." The third paradox appears when we take "time" to be independently real. If we maintain the proper pattern of "distance and time," then the paradoxes disappear.

---

[1] Some invoke infinite series convergence, continuity of space, continuity of time, relativity space-time, quantum uncertainty principle, etc. These proposals all treat time and space as two separate and independent objects.

Zeno paradoxes seem to validate Parmenides' key statement: "": "They have established (the custom of) naming two forms, but the *unity* behind the two opposites ought to be (mentioned): that is where they have gone astray."[1]

Dichotomy Paradox

In dichotomy, if the distance to run is divided in half, the trip must reach the first half. But before the trip can reach the first half, it must travel the half of the first half. Hence, by dividing the distance indefinitely, the trip cannot even begin. The paradoxical conclusion that travels over any finite distance can neither be completed nor begun and so all motion must be an illusion.

Dichotomy involves repeatedly splitting a distance into two parts and reaching an apparent conclusion of motionlessness.

Systems Thinking Proposal

The system has two objects: distance and time. The speed of the traveler is a pattern of distance over time. The paradox appears when we take the distance as an independent object. The pattern of speed is ignored.

---

[1] It is clear that the two forms refer to the way we contrast everything with two opposites. If we accept the observation made by Gadamer in the meaning of the Greek word "*mia*" should mean "*unity*" instead of just "one," then the paragraph becomes unambiguous and consistent.

In the paradox, the distance is decreased but the time period is not decreased. The distance is infinitely decreased; however, the corresponding time period is not proportionally decreased. Thus, the speed of the traveler is becoming zero when the distance is infinitely small. Of course, the traveler cannot travel any distance with a speed of zero.

The essential pattern of the system is *speed* itself. Taking the object *distance* as an independent reality fragment the wholeness of the system. If the speed had been kept constant, then the paradox can be avoided.

For example, if it takes 10 seconds to go across the room, then half the distance would mean 5 seconds, and so on. The conclusion is that: at time zero, the motion has not begun. Thinking at the systems level will avoid such a paradox.

Achilles and the tortoise

In the paradox of Achilles and the Tortoise, Achilles is in a footrace with the tortoise. If we assume that Achilles allows the tortoise a head start of 100 meters, Achilles will never be able to overtake the tortoise.

Each racer starts running at some constant speed. Achilles is very fast and the tortoise is very slow. After some finite time, Achilles will have run 100 meters, bringing him to the tortoise's starting point. During this time, the tortoise has run a much shorter distance, say, 10 meters. It will then take Achilles some further time to run that distance, by which time the tortoise will have advanced farther; and then Achilles needs more time still to reach this third point, while the tortoise moves further ahead.

Thus, whenever Achilles reaches somewhere the tortoise has been, he still has further to go. Therefore, because Achilles must reach where the tortoise has already been, he can never overtake the tortoise.

Systems Thinking Proposal

The system consists of a fast runner, a slow runner, and a head-start distance of 100 meters. The three objects are the head-start distance and two speeds. The running speeds are the patterns of the systems.

In the paradox, the attention is directed to the object of the head-start *distance* alone. When Achilles reaches a distance, the tortoise moves a further distance. This scenario repeats itself and Achilles can never overtake the tortoise.

The relative speeds of the two runners are major characteristics of the system but are ignored in the analysis of the system. The paradox appears because we take an object (the head-start distance or distance) as an independent reality and fail to maintain the wholeness of the system. This is against the key statement of Parmenides.

In this example, the tortoise is ahead of Achilles by 100 meters. If Achilles runs 20 meters per second and the tortoise 10 meters per second, then it will take 5 seconds. If speed is included in the analysis, the total time in the paradox covers the first 10 seconds only, during which time, Achilles is always behind the tortoise. When the time period is longer than 10 seconds, Achilles will be ahead.

Distance	Tortoise at 10 m/s	Achilles at 20 m/s
100m	5s moves by 50m	5s moves by 100m
50	2.5s moves by 25 m	2.5s moves by 50m
25	1.25s moves by 12.5m	1.25s moves by 25m
…	…	…
0	10s	10s

We go astray in this paradox when we decouple "distance in-between" from the reality of speed differences. When time is taken into consideration, we recover the reality of speed.

Arrow-in-Flight Paradox

In the arrow paradox, Zeno states that for a motion to occur, an object must change the position which it occupies. He states that in any one instant of time, the arrow is neither moving to where it is, nor to where it is not. It cannot move to where it is not, because no time elapses for it to move there; it cannot move to where it is, because it is already there. In other words, at every instant of time, there is no motion occurring. If everything is motionless at every instant, then motion is impossible.

Systems Thinking Proposal

The speed is the pattern that represents the reality in this system. The system consists of a moving arrow of a certain speed. The objects are the position and the time associated with the arrow. The pattern is that the change in position and the change in time are interrelated by the speed of the arrow.

The paradox is due to our action of taking the time and the space as independent "real" objects. When we look at a point in time, the speed of the arrow is essentially taken into zero at that point, since the arrow either terminates at or originates from that point. The pattern of speed is ignored at each point. In this case, the arrow is motionless.

In the systems view, the changes of position and time are interrelated as the speed of the arrow. When this networked pattern is not preserved, a paradox will appear.

Appendix C: Keywords

The model of the whole system is shown in Figure 2. For clarification, we adhere to the following definitions of the terms often used in systems thinking.

- Parts – Parts generally refer to the objects or the subsystems, excluding their interactions with their environment. The whole system is the organization of these parts. Any part can be further subdivided. In our model, parts do not have formal definitions.
- Objects - An object is the smallest unit in the subsystems. Parts may have their abstract definitions or properties by comparing to other parts. They have relative meanings only. The objects form patterns in the subsystems. An object is bare, i.e., *without* interactions with other objects.
- Subsystems – Each subsystem has a boundary, outside of which is its environment. The environment shows the constraints imposed on the subsystem to support the function of the whole system. The environment is due to residual interactions between the subsystem and other subsystems. A subsystem is an open system interacting with all other subsystems.

- Final Subsystems or Actualities – When a subsystem is fully integrated with all interactions, the subsystem has no environment. It becomes free and independent. The patterns of the final subsystems should reflect the properties of the whole system.
- The System – The highest level only specifies the properties of the system. It serves as a principle in the discussions of the system. This level is transcendental to the realm of analysis. The principle is Oneness that needs to be preserved at all levels.
- Patterns - A pattern generally refers to the pattern of the objects.
- Reality – A reality is a living system, where reality is independent and free. It is based on the wholeness and Oneness of the system.

REFERENCES

1. Capra, Fritjof, and Luisi, Pier Luigi, *The Systems View of Life*: A Unifying Vision, Cambridge University Press, Cambridge, 2014.
2. Von Bertalanffy, Ludwig, *General System Theory*, George Braziller, New York, 2015
3. *Alexander Bogdanov and the Origins of Systems Thinking in Russia*, Editors John Biggart, Peter Dudley, and Francis King, Avebury, 1998
4. Wang, Wayne L. *Dynamic Tao and Its Manifestations,* Helena Island Publisher, Darien, Illinois, 2004, 2016 revised.
5. Wang, Wayne L., *The Logic of Tao Philosophy,* Helena Island Publisher, Darien, Illinois, 2013
6. Wang, Wayne L., *Tao Te Ching: an Ultimate Translation*, Helena Island Publisher, Darien, Illinois, 2013

INDEX

THE AUTHOR

Wayne L. Wang was born in Taiwan and migrated to the U.S. for his graduate studies in engineering and physics. In 1971, Dr. Wang received his Ph. D. degree from the Massachusetts Institute of Technology. He researched a theoretical physicist, nuclear reactor safety research, mobile and data telecommunication systems. He retired in 2010 and continues to work on the logic of Tao philosophy.

His first book on this subject, *Dynamic Tao and Its Manifestations* shows the intimate similarities between Tao Philosophy and Quantum Cosmology. His second book, *The Logic of Tao Philosophy*, brings forward a clear logic structure of Tao. His third book is a logical translation of the Chinese classic, *The Tao Te Ching: An Ultimate Translation*. He also discusses religions, psychotherapy, and ancient philosophy in *Searching for the Meaning of Life*.

He has published seven books as the *Searching for Tao Series*. This book, *Systems Thinking and Logic of Tao Philosophy*, is a major summary of the Series. His analysis of Tao Philosophy will set a new framework for modern Tao studies, in both the Eastern and the Western arenas.

Website: http://dynamictaos.com
For ordering information, updates, and available services, please visit our website or send an email to the author. Email: wayne.wang@hotmail.com

www.ingramcontent.com/pod-product-compliance
Lightning Source LLC
Chambersburg PA
CBHW072004040426
42447CB00009B/1479